HC

Campo Santo

Campo Santo

W. G. SEBALD

Edited by Sven Meyer
Translated by Anthea Bell

HAMISH HAMILTON
an imprint of
PENGUIN BOOKS

HAMISH HAMILTON LTD

Published by the Penguin Group
Penguin Books Ltd, 80 Strand, London WC2R 0RL, England
Penguin Group (USA), Inc., 375 Hudson Street, New York, New York 10014, USA
Penguin Books Australia Ltd, 250 Camberwell Road,
Camberwell, Victoria 3124, Australia
Penguin Books Canada Ltd, 10 Alcorn Avenue, Toronto, Ontario, Canada M4V 3B2
Penguin Books India (P) Ltd, 11 Community Centre,
Panchsheel Park, New Delhi – 110 017, India
Penguin Group (NZ), cnr Airborne and Rosedale Roads, Albany, Auckland 1310, New Zealand
Penguin Books (South Africa) (Pty) Ltd, 24 Sturdee Avenue,
Rosebank 2196, South Africa

Penguin Books Ltd, Registered Offices: 80 Strand, London WC2R 0RL

www.penguin.com

This translation first published 2005

1

Copyright © the Estate of W. G. Sebald, 2005
Translation copyright © Anthea Bell, 2005

The moral right of the author has been asserted

Set in 12.5/17.5 pt Monotype Perpetua
Typeset by Rowland Phototypesetting Ltd, Bury St Edmunds, Suffolk
Printed in Great Britain by Clays Ltd, St Ives plc

A CIP catalogue record for this book is available from the British Library

ISBN 0-241-14277-6

Publisher's Note

Campo Santo brings together pieces written over a period of some twenty years touching, in typical Sebaldian fashion, on a variety of subjects. None has been previously published in book form, but the ideas expressed in 'Between History and Natural History' will be familiar to some readers – the essay is the predecessor of the Zürich lectures which later became the backbone of *On the Natural History of Destruction*.

Contents

Foreword   ix

Prose

A Little Excursion to Ajaccio   3

Campo Santo   16

The Alps in the Sea   36

La cour de l'ancienne école   49

Essays

Strangeness, Integration and Crisis:
On Peter Handke's play *Kaspar*   55

Between History and Natural History:
On the literary description of total
destruction   68

Constructs of Mourning: Günter Grass
and Wolfgang Hildesheimer   102

Des Häschens Kind, der kleine Has: On the
poet Ernst Herbeck's totem animal   130

To the Brothel by way of Switzerland:
On Kafka's travel diaries   140

Dream Textures: A brief note on
Nabokov   146

Kafka Goes to the Movies   156

Scomber scombrus, or the Common
Mackerel: On pictures by Jan Peter
Tripp   174

The Mystery of the Red-brown Skin:
An approach to Bruce Chatwin   179

Moments musicaux   188

An Attempt at Restitution   206

Acceptance Speech to the Collegium of
the German Academy   216

Notes   218

Sources   227

Foreword

Campo Santo is a collection of prose by W. G. Sebald, who died in a road accident on 14 December 2001. His novel *Austerlitz* had been published shortly before, and Sebald had not yet begun working on a new book since finishing it. However, there was a work that was never finished: in the middle of the 1990s, after the publication of *The Rings of Saturn* (1995), Sebald began writing a book about Corsica, but then left it on one side and turned to writing essays and working on *Austerlitz*. Parts of this Corsica project were published from 1996 onwards as separate pieces, in various places; Sebald also used a long section in 2000 as a text for his speech on the occasion of the award of the Düsseldorf Heine Prize. These pieces are collected together for the first time and arranged in order of their composition in the opening section of the present volume. 'A Little Excursion to Ajaccio' ('In September last year, during a two-week holiday on the island of Corsica'), 'Campo Santo' ('My first walk on the day after my arrival in Piana'), 'The Alps in the Sea' ('Once upon a time Corsica was entirely covered by forest') and finally the miniature '*La cour de l'ancienne école*'. Together, the four Corsican pieces, each self-contained, make up admittedly only an incomplete spectrum which cannot show exactly what the abandoned book would have been like; however, collecting the separate parts makes them appear in a new light, and they also cast light on each other. Sebald's literary estate, which has not yet been studied and edited, contains no other recent literary works. The Corsican project is the last and unfinished work of a writer's life that came to a premature end.

The second part of this volume illustrates Sebald's other side, as essayist and critic. Two collections of essays on Austrian literature, *Die Beschreibung des Unglücks* (1985) and *Unheimiche Heimat* (1991) have already been published in German. In addition, there are the later volumes *Logis in einem Landhaus* (1998) and *Luftkrieg und Literatur* (1999),* including an essay on Alfred Andersch which has provoked much controversy. The development shown in these volumes is also reflected in the essays in the present collection, which are chronologically arranged. They have previously appeared in

*Published in English as *On the Natural History of Destruction*, and also including the essays on Jean Améry and Peter Weiss, which in the original German are part of the present volume published by Hanser.

scholarly journals, literary magazines and the arts sections of newspapers, but are now published in book form for the first time. There are early works of literary criticism – the first, on Peter Handke's play *Kaspar*, dates from 1975 – which already show Sebald's concern with such subjects as destruction, mourning and memory, themes around which his literary work would continue to revolve, as well as the development of his stylistic individuality. The later essays – on Ernst Herbeck, Vladimir Nabokov, Franz Kafka, Jan Peter Tripp and Bruce Chatwin – written from the early 1990s onward at the same time as the narratives *Vertigo*, *The Emigrants*, *The Rings of Saturn* and *Austerlitz*, finally dispense with footnotes, throw the ballast of scholarly references overboard and instead strike the typically Sebaldian note. In '*Moments musicaux*' and 'An Attempt at Restitution', Sebald's speeches at the opening of the Munich Opera Festival and the Stuttgart House of Literature in the year of his death, the essayist can no longer be distinguished from the writer. In his final works Sebald practised the principle to which he had confessed in an interview with Sigrid Löffler in 1993: 'My medium is prose, not the novel.' At the end of the volume is Sebald's speech accepting membership of the German Academy for Language and Literature. Here he tells us of a dream in which he, like Johann Peter Hebel before him, is 'unmasked as a traitor to his country and a fraud' – in view of such fears, he says, he regards admission to the Academy as an 'unhoped-for form of justification'. Another, perhaps less unanticipated and certainly no less honourable form of justification is the wide acceptance of Sebald's books by the general reader and the serious discussion of his ideas.

Sven Meyer

Prose

A Little Excursion to Ajaccio

In September last year, during a two-week holiday on the island of Corsica, I took a blue bus one day down the west coast to Ajaccio to spend a little time looking round the town, of which I knew nothing except that it was the birthplace of the Emperor Napoleon. It was a beautiful, sunlit day, the branches of the palms in the Place Maréchal-Foch moved gently in a breeze coming in off the sea, a snow-white cruise ship lay in the harbour like a great iceberg, and I wandered through the streets feeling carefree and at ease, now and then going into one of the dark, tunnel-like entrances of buildings to read the names of their unknown inhabitants on the metal letter boxes with a certain rapt attention, trying to imagine what it would be like to live in one of these stone citadels, occupied to my life's end solely with the study of time past and passing. But since we can none of us really live entirely withdrawn into ourselves, and must all have some more or less significant design in view, my wishful thinking about a few last years with no duties of any kind soon gave way to a need to fill the present afternoon somehow, and so I found myself, hardly knowing how I came there, in the entrance hall of the Musée Fesch, with notebook and pencil and a ticket in my hand.

Joseph Fesch, as I later read on looking him up in my old *Guide Bleu*, was the son of the late second marriage of Letizia Bonaparte's mother to a Swiss military officer in Genoese service, and was thus Napoleon's step-uncle. At the beginning of his career in the Church he held a minor ecclesiastical position in Ajaccio. After his nephew had appointed him Archbishop of Lyon and envoy to the Holy See, however, he became one of the most insatiable art collectors of his day, a time when the market was positively flooded with paintings and artefacts taken from churches, monasteries and palaces during the French Revolution, bought from *émigrés*, and looted in the plundering of Dutch and Italian cities.

Fesch's aim was no less than to document the entire course of European art history in his private collection. No one knows for certain just how many pictures he actually owned, but the number is thought to be around thirty thousand. Among those that, after his death in 1838 and some devious manoeuvres on the part of Joseph Bonaparte as executor of the Cardinal's will, found their way into the museum especially built for them in Ajaccio are a Madonna by Cosimo Tura, Botticelli's *Virgin Under a Garland*, Pier Francesco Cittadini's *Still Life with Turkish Carpet*, Spadino's *Garden Fruits with Parrot*, Titian's *Portrait of a Young Man with a Glove*, and a number of other wonderful paintings.

The finest of all, it seemed to me that afternoon, was a picture by Pietro Paolini, who lived and worked in Lucca in the seventeenth century. It shows a woman of perhaps thirty against a deep black background that lightens to a very dark brown only towards the left-hand side of the painting. She has large, melancholy eyes and wears a dress the colour of the night, which does not stand out from the surrounding darkness even by suggestion and is thus really invisible, and yet it is present in every fold and drape of its fabric. She wears a string of pearls around her neck. Her right arm protectively embraces her small daughter, who stands in front of her, turning sideways towards the edge of the picture, but with her grave face, upon which the tears have only just dried, turned towards the observer in a kind of silent challenge. The little girl wears a brick-red dress, and the soldier doll hardly three inches high which she is holding out to us, whether in memory of her father who has gone to war or to ward off the evil eye we may be casting on her, also wears red. I stood in front of this double portrait for a long time, seeing in it, as I thought at the time, an annulment of all the unfathomable misfortune of life.

Before leaving the museum I went down to the basement, where there is a collection of Napoleonic mementoes and devotional items on display. It includes objects adorned with the head and initials of Napoleon – letter openers, seals, penknives, tobacco and snuff boxes – miniatures of the entire clan and most of their descendants, silhouettes and biscuit medallions, an ostrich egg painted with an Egyptian scene, brightly coloured faience plates, porcelain cups, plaster busts, alabaster figures, a bronze of Bonaparte mounted on a dromedary and also, beneath a glass dome almost as tall as a man, a moth-eaten uniform tunic cut like a tailcoat, edged with red braid and bearing twelve brass buttons – *l'habit d'un colonel des Chasseurs de la Garde, que porta Napoléon Ier* ('the uniform of a colonel in the Chasseurs de la Garde, worn by Napoleon I').

There are also many statuettes of the Emperor carved from soapstone and ivory and showing him in familiar poses, the tallest about ten centimetres high and each of the others smaller than the last, until the smallest seems almost nothing but a white speck, perhaps representing the vanishing point of human history. One of these diminutive figures depicts Napoleon after his abdication *'sur le rocher de l'île de Sainte-Hélène'* ('on the rock of the island of St Helena'). Scarcely larger than a pea, he sits in cloak and three-cornered hat astride a tiny chair set on a fragment of tuff which really does come from his place of exile, and he is gazing out into the distance with furrowed brow. He cannot have felt at ease there in the middle of the bleak Atlantic, and he must have missed the excitement of his past life, particularly as it seems that he could not really depend even on the few faithful souls who still surrounded him in his isolation.

Or so at least we might conclude from an article in *Corse-Matin* published on the day of my visit to the Musée Fesch, in which a certain Professor René Maury claimed that a study of several hairs from the Emperor's head undertaken in the FBI laboratories established beyond any doubt '*que Napoléon a lentement été empoisonné à l'arsenic à Sainte-Hélène, entre 1817 et 1821, par l'un de ses compagnons d'exil, le comte de Montholon, sur l'instigation de sa femme Albine qui était devenue la maîtresse de l'empereur et s'est trouvée enceinte de lui*' ('that Napoleon was slowly poisoned with arsenic on St Helena, between 1817 and 1821, by one of his companions in exile, the Comte de Montholon, at the urging of his wife Albine, who had become the Emperor's mistress and was pregnant by him'). I do not really know what we should think of such stories. The Napoleonic myth has, after all, given rise to the most astonishing tales, always said to be based on incontrovertible fact. Kafka, for instance, tells us that on 11 November 1911 he attended a *conférence* in the Rudolfinum on the subject of *La Légende de Napoléon*, at which one Richepin, a sturdy man of fifty with a fine

7

figure, his hair arranged in stiff whorls in the Daudet style and lying close to his scalp, said among other things that in the past Napoleon's tomb used to be opened once a year so that old soldiers filing past could set eyes on their embalmed Emperor. But later the custom of the annual opening of the tomb was discontinued, because his face was becoming rather green and bloated. Richepin himself as a child, however, says Kafka, had seen the dead Emperor in the arms of his great-uncle, who had served in Africa and for whom the commandant had the tomb specially opened. Moreover, Kafka's diary entry continues, the *conférence* concluded with the speaker swearing that even in a thousand years' time every mote of the dust of his own corpse, should it have consciousness, would still be ready to follow the call of Napoleon.

After I had left the Musée Fesch I sat for a while on a stone bench in the Place Letizia, which is really just a small garden set among tall buildings and containing some trees, with eucalyptus and oleanders, fan palms, laurels and myrtles forming an oasis in the middle of the town. This garden is separated from the street by iron railings, and the whitewashed façade of the Casa Bonaparte stands on the other side of the road. The flag of the Republic hung over the gateway through which a more or less steady stream of visitors was going in and coming out: Dutch and Germans, Belgians and French,

Austrians and Italians, and once a whole group of elderly Japanese of very distinguished appearance. Most of them had left, and the afternoon was already drawing to an end, when I finally entered the building. The dimly lit entrance hall was deserted, and there seemed to be no one at the ticket desk either. Only when I was right in front of the counter, and was just putting out my hand to one of the picture postcards displayed there, did I see a young woman sitting, or I could almost have said lying behind it, in a black leather office armchair tipped backward.

I actually had to look down at her over the edge of the counter, and this act of looking down at the cashier of the Casa Bonaparte, who was probably only tired from much standing and perhaps had just dozed off, was one of those moments strangely experienced in slow motion that are sometimes remembered years later. When the cashier rose she proved to be a lady of very stately proportions. You could imagine her on an operatic stage, exhausted by the drama of her life, singing 'Lasciate mi morir' or some such closing aria. Far more striking, however, than her diva-like figure, and something that became clear only at second glance but was all the more startling for that, was her resemblance to the French emperor in whose birthplace she acted as doorkeeper.

She had the same rounded face, the same large, very

protuberant eyes, the same dun-coloured hair falling in a jagged fringe over her forehead. As she gave me my ticket and saw that I could not take my eyes off her, she gave me a forbearing smile and said, in positively seductive tones, that the tour of the house began on the second floor. I climbed the black marble staircase, and was not a little surprised to be met on the top landing by another lady who also seemed to be of Napoleonic descent, or rather who somehow reminded me of Masséna or Mack or another of the legendary marshals of France, probably because I had always imagined them as a race of dwarfish heroes.

For the lady awaiting me at the top of the stairs was of strikingly small stature, a feature further accentuated by her short neck and her very short arms, which scarcely reached her hips. In addition, she wore the hues of the tricolour: a blue skirt and a white blouse, and around her waist a red belt with a heavy, gleaming brass buckle which had something decidedly military about it. When I had reached the top step the Maréchale stepped aside, half-turning, and said, 'Bonjour, monsieur'. She too wore a slightly ironic smile, indicating, as I thought, that she knew far more than I could ever guess. Rather disconcerted by my encounter with these two discreet messengers from the past, which I could not account for to myself, I wandered aimlessly around the rooms for a while, went down to the first floor, and then climbed back up to the second floor again. Only gradually did I make sense of the furnishings of the place and the items on display.

On the whole everything was still as Flaubert had described it in the diary of his visit to Corsica: rather unassuming rooms furnished in the style of the Republic; a few chandeliers and mirrors of Venetian glass, the looking-glasses now spotted and dim; a soft twilight, for the tall double windows were wide open, just as they had been in Flaubert's time, but the dark green slatted blinds had been closed. Sunlight lay in white stripes like a ladder on the oak floorboards. It was as if not an hour had passed since Flaubert's visit. Of the items he mentioned, only the imperial cloak with the golden bees that he had seen shining in the chiaroscuro was no longer here. Family documents inscribed in handsomely curving letters lay quiet in their glass cases, with Carlo Bonaparte's two shotguns, a couple of pistols and a fencing foil.

On the walls hung cameos and other miniatures, a series of coloured steel engravings of the battles of Friedland, Marengo and Austerlitz, and a genealogical tree of the Bonaparte family in a heavy frame covered with gold leaf, in front of which I finally stopped. A huge oak towered up from the brown earth against a sky-blue background, and hanging from its twigs and branches were little white clouds cut from paper, bearing the names and dates of all members of the imperial house and the later descendants of the Napoleonic clan. They were all assembled here: the King of Naples, the King of Rome and the King of Westphalia, Marianne Elisa, Maria Annunciata and Marie Pauline, the most beautiful and light-hearted of the seven siblings, the unfortunate Duke of Reichstadt, the ornithologist and ichthyologist Charles·Lucien, Plon-Plon, son of Jérôme, and Mathilde Letizia, his daughter, Napoleon III with his twirled moustache, the Bonapartes of Baltimore and many more.

Without my noticing the Maréchale Ney had come up beside me, perhaps seeing my obvious emotion as I examined this genealogical work of art, and told me in a reverent whisper that this *création unique* had been made towards the end of the last century by the daughter of a notary in Corte who was a great admirer of Napoleon. The leaves and sprays of flowers adorned with a few butterflies at the bottom of the picture, said Madame la Maréchale, were genuine dried plants from the maquis, sempervivums, myrtles and rosemary, and the dark, sinuous tree trunk standing out in relief against the blue background was braided from the girl's own hair. Whether out of love for the Emperor or for her father, she must have devoted endless hours to her work.

I nodded attentively at this explanation, and stayed there for some time longer before I turned, left the room and went down to the first floor, where the

Bonaparte family had lived after they first came to Ajaccio. Carlo Bonaparte, Napoleon's father, was secretary to Pasquale Paoli,* and after the defeat of the patriots at Corte in their unequal struggle against the French troops he had moved to the seaport of Ajaccio for safety's sake. Accompanied by Letizia, who was pregnant with Napoleon at the time, he travelled through the wild mountains and ravines of the interior, and I imagine that the two tiny figures riding their mules through that overwhelming panorama, or sitting alone by a small camp fire in the darkness of the night, must have resembled Mary and Joseph in one of the many depictions that have come down to us of the Flight into Egypt. At any event, if there is anything in the theory of prenatal experience, then this dramatic journey explains a good deal about the character of the future Emperor, not least the fact that he always did everything with a certain precipitate haste, even in the matter of his own birth, when he was in such a hurry that Letizia was unable to reach her bed and had to bring him into the world on a sofa in what is known as the Yellow Room.

Perhaps it was with these remarkable circumstances attending the beginning of his life in mind that Napoleon later made his beloved mother a present of a Nativity scene in rather doubtful taste, carved from ivory and

*Pasquale Paoli (1725–1807) was known as the 'Father of the Corsican Nation'. He drew up the constititution of Corsica.

still on view at the Casa Bonaparte. During the 1770s and 1780s, while the Corsicans were adjusting to the new regime, neither Letizia nor Carlo can of course have dreamed that the children who sat at the dining table with them daily would eventually rise to the rank of kings and queens, or that the time would come when the most hot-tempered of them, young Ribulione, a lad always involved in local street fights, would wear the crown of a vast empire extending over almost the whole of Europe.

But what can we know in advance of the course of history, which unfolds according to some logically indecipherable law, impelled forward, often changing direction at the crucial moment, by tiny, imponderable events, by a barely perceptible current of air, a leaf falling to the ground, a glance exchanged across a great crowd of people? Even in retrospect we cannot see what things were really like before that moment, and how this or that world-shaking event came about. The most precise study of the past scarcely comes any closer to the unimaginable truth than, for instance, a far-fetched claim such as I once heard made by an amateur historian called Alfonse Huyghens, who lived in the capital of Belgium and had been pursuing his research on Napoleon for years; according to him, all the cataclysmic events caused by the Emperor of the French in the lands and realms of Europe were to be traced solely to his colour-blindness, which made him unable to tell red from green. The more blood flowed on the battlefield, this Belgian scholar told me, the greener Napoleon thought the grass was growing.

In the evening I walked along the Cours Napoléon, and then sat for two hours in a small restaurant not far from the Gare Maritime with a view of the white cruise ship. Over coffee I studied the advertisements in the local paper and wondered whether to go to the cinema. I like to visit the cinema in foreign towns, but neither *Judge Dredd* at the Empire, *USS Alabama* at the Bonaparte nor *L'Amour à tout prix* at the Laetitia seemed to me the right way to end this day. At about ten, therefore, I was back in the hotel where I had taken a room late that morning. I opened the windows and looked out over the rooftops of the town. Traffic was still driving down the streets, but suddenly everything fell silent, just for a few seconds, until one of those bombs that frequently go off in Corsica exploded with a short, sharp bang, obviously only a few streets away. I lay down and soon fell asleep, with the sound of the firefighters' sirens howling in my ears.

Campo Santo

My first walk on the day after my arrival in Piana took me out on a road that soon begins falling away steeply in terrifying curves, sharp bends and zigzags, leading past almost vertical rocky precipices densely overgrown by green scrub, and so down to the bottom of a ravine opening out into the Bay of Ficajola several hundred metres below. Down there, where until well into the post-war period a community of twelve or so fisher-folk lived in dwellings roughly cobbled together and roofed with corrugated iron, some of which now have their doors and windows boarded up, I spent half the afternoon with a few other tourists from Marseille, Munich or Milan who had installed themselves with their picnics and assorted items of practical equipment in couples or family groups, at regular distances from each other, and I lay motionless for a long time by the little quicksilver stream that even now, at the end of summer, ran constantly down over the last granite steps of the valley floor, with that proverbial babble familiar to me from some dim and distant past, only to give up the ghost without a sound on the beach and seep away. I watched the sand martins circling the flame-coloured cliffs high above in astonishingly large numbers, soaring from the bright side of the rocks into the shadows and darting out of the shadows into the light again, and once that afternoon, which for me was filled with a sense of liberation and appeared to stretch endlessly away in every direction, I swam out to sea with a great sense of lightness, very far out, so far that I felt I could simply let myself drift away into the evening and so into the night. But as soon as, obeying the strange instinct that binds us to life, I turned back after all and made for the land which, from this distance, resembled a foreign continent, swimming became more and more difficult with every stroke, and not as if I were labouring against the current that had been carrying me on before; no, I was inclined to think that I was swimming steadily uphill, if one can say so of a stretch of water. The view before my eyes seemed to have tipped out of its frame, was leaning towards me, swaying and flickering of its own accord, with the upper rim of the picture skewed several degrees in my direction and the lower rim skewed away from me to the same extent. And sometimes I felt as if the prospect towering so menacingly in front of me was not a part of the real world but the reproduction of a now insuperable inner faintness, turned inside out and shot through with blue-black markings. Even harder than reaching the shore was the climb later up the winding road and the barely trodden paths which here and there link one curve in the road to the next in a direct line. Although I placed one foot in front of the other only slowly and very steadily, the afternoon heat building up between the rock walls very soon brought sweat running down my forehead, and the blood pulsed in my neck as it did in the throats of the lizards sitting everywhere in my path, frozen in mid-movement with fear. It took me a good hour and a half to climb to Piana again, but once there I could walk as if weightlessly, like a man who has mastered the art of levitation, past the first houses and gardens and along the wall of the plot of land where the local people bury their dead. When I passed through the iron gate, which squealed on its hinges, this proved to be a rather desolate graveyard of the kind not uncommon in France, where you have the impression not so much of an antechamber to eternal life as of a place administered by the local authority and designed for the secular removal of waste matter from human society. Many of the graves standing in untidy rows all over the dry slope, their lines everywhere broken or slightly displaced, have already sunk into the ground, and are partially overlapped by later additions. Hesitantly, and with that touch of reluctance that one feels even today in approaching the dead too closely, I clambered over crumbling plinths and edgings, tombstones shifted out of place, ruinous masonry, a crucifix fallen from its mount and disfigured by rust marks, a leaden urn, an angel's hand – silent fragments of a town abandoned years ago, and not a shrub or a tree to give shade anywhere, no thujas or cypresses of the kind so often planted in southern cemeteries, whether for comfort or as a sign of mourning. At first sight I really believed that the only reminders in the Piana graveyard of the nature which, we have always hoped, will endure long after our own end, were the artificial purple, mauve and pink flowers obviously pressed upon their customers by French undertakers, made of silk or nylon chiffon, of brightly painted porcelain, wire and metal, appearing not so much a sign of enduring affection as the final emergence of a kind of proof that, despite all assurances to the contrary, we offer our dead only the cheapest substitutes for the diverse beauty of life. Not until I looked more carefully around me did I notice the weeds – the vetch, wild thyme, white clover, yarrow and camomile, cow wheat, yellow oat grass, and many other grasses with names unknown to me – that had grown around the stones to form actual herbariums and miniature landscapes, still showing some green but already half dead, and far lovelier, I thought to myself, than the ornamental funerary plants sold by German cemetery florists, usually consisting of heathers, dwarf conifers and pansies of absolutely standard shape, planted in spot-less, soot-black soil in strict geometrical rows, as I still see them in unwelcome memories of my now distant childhood and youth in the foothills of the Alps. But here and there among the thin flower stems, the blades and ears of grass in the graveyard of Piana, a departed soul looked out from one of those oval sepia portraits set in thin gilded frames which until the sixties used to be placed on graves in Mediterranean countries: a blond hussar in his high-collared uniform tunic; a girl who died on her nineteenth birthday, her face almost extinguished by the sun and the rain; a short-necked man with his tie in a large knot, who had been a colonial civil servant in Oran until 1958; a little soldier, forage cap tilted side-ways on his head, who came home badly wounded from the futile defence of the jungle fortress of Dien Bien Phuh. In many places weeds already cover the polished marble votive tablets on the newer graves, most of which bear only the brief inscription 'Regrets' or 'Regrets éternels' in neatly curving characters which might have been copied by a child from a manual of handwriting. 'Regrets éternels' – like almost all the phrases in which we express our feelings for those who have gone before, it is not without ambiguity, for not only does the announcement of the everlasting inconsolability of the bereaved confine itself to the absolute minimum, it also sounds, if one stops to consider it, almost like an admission to the dead of guilt, a half-hearted request for forbearance made to those laid in the earth before their time. Only the names of the dead themselves seemed to me clear and free of any ambiguity, not a few of them being as perfect in both significance and sound as if those who once bore them had been saints in their own lifetime, or messengers from a distant world devised by our higher yearnings, visiting this one only for a brief guest performance. Yet in reality they too, those who had borne the names Gregorio Grimaldi, Angelina Bonavita, Natale Nicoli, Santo Santini, Serafino Fontano and Archangelo Casabianca, had certainly not been proof against human malice, their own or that of others. Another striking feature of the design of the Piana graveyard, and one that revealed itself only gradually as I walked among the graves, was the fact that in general the dead were buried in clans, so that the Ceccaldi lay beside the Ceccaldi and the Quilichini beside the Quilichini, but this old order, founded on not many more than a dozen names, had been forced some time ago to give way to the order of modern civil life, in which everyone is alone and in the end is allotted a place only for himself and his closest relations, one which corresponds as accurately as possible to the size of his property or the depth of his poverty. If one cannot speak of a wealth of ostentatious funerary architecture anywhere in the small communities of Corsica, even a place like the Piana graveyard has a few tombs adorned with pediments where the more prosperous have found an appropriate final resting place. The next social class down is represented by sarcophagus-like structures made of granite or concrete slabs, depending on the assets of those laid to rest there. Stone slabs lie on the ground above the graves of the dead of even less importance. And those whose means are insufficient even for such a slab must be content with turquoise or pink gravel kept in place by a narrow border around it, while the very poor have only a metal cross stuck in the bare earth, or a crucifix roughly welded from tubing, perhaps painted bronze or with a gold cord wound around it. In this way the graveyard of Piana, a place where until recently only the more or less poverty-stricken lived, now resembles the necropolises of our great cities in reflecting all gradations of the social hierarchy as marked by the unequal division of earthly riches. The biggest stones are usually rolled over the graves of the richest people, for it is to be feared that they are the most likely to begrudge their progeny their inheritance, and to try to take back what they have lost. The mighty blocks of stone erected above them for the sake of security are of course, with self-deluding cunning, disguised as monuments of deep veneration. Significantly, such expense is unnecessary on the death of one of our lesser brethren, who can perhaps call nothing his own at the hour of his death but the suit in which he is buried, or so I thought as I gazed out over the highest-standing row of graves, looking across the Piana cemetery and the silver crowns of the olive trees beyond the wall, and so on to the Gulf of Porto shining up from far below. Something that particularly surprised me about this resting place of the dead was that not one of the funerary inscriptions was more than sixty or seventy years old. I discovered some months later that the reason lay in one of those strange Corsican situations involving blood feuds and banditry, finding this information in what I consider in many respects a model study by Stephen Wilson, one of my professional colleagues, who presents the extensive material he has assembled during many years of research to his readers with the greatest imaginable care, clarity and restraint.* The absence of any dates of death going back even to the early twentieth century was not, as I had at first suspected, to be accounted for by the now very usual practice of successively abandoning old graves, nor could it be explained by the existence of an earlier graveyard somewhere else; rather, the reason was simply that graveyards in Corsica were made official burial places only around the middle of the nineteenth century, and even then it was a long time before the

*Feuding Conflict and Banditry in 19th Century Corsica (Cambridge University Press, 1988).

23

population accepted them. In an account dating from 1893, for instance, we hear that no one used the Ajaccio town cemetery apart from the poor and the Protestants, who were known as *luterani*. To all appearances, the bereaved were unwilling to remove the dead who owned a piece of land from their hereditary property, or else they dared not do so. For centuries the usual form of Corsican burial, on land inherited from the forefathers of the dead, was like a contract affirming inalienable rights to that land, a contract between every dead man and his progeny, tacitly renewed from generation to generation. You therefore find little dwellings for the dead everywhere, *da paese a paese*: burial chambers and mausoleums, here under a chestnut tree, there in an olive grove full of moving light and shade, in the middle of a pumpkin bed, in a field of oats or on a hillside overgrown with the feathery foliage of yellow-green dill. In such places, which are often particularly beautiful and have a good view over the family's territory, the village and the rest of the local land, the dead were always in a way at home, were not sent into exile and could continue to watch over the boundaries of their property. I also read, in a source which I cannot now place, that many old Corsican women used to go out to the dwellings of the dead after the day's work was done, to listen to what they had to say and consult them on the cultivation of the land and other matters to do with the correct conduct of life. For a long time, when landless people died – shepherds, day labourers, Italian farm workers and other indigent folk – they were simply sewn into sacks and thrown down a shaft with a lid over it. Such a communal grave, where the corpses probably lay all jumbled up like cabbages and turnips, was called an *arca*, and in many places it might alternatively be a stone house without any windows or doors, the dead being pushed down inside it through a hole in the roof which could be reached by stairs going up the outside wall. And in the Campodonico near Orezza, Stephen Wilson tells us, those who owned no land were just thrown down a ravine, a practice which the bandit Muzzarettu, who died in 1952 at the age of eighty-five, said was still usual even when he lived in Grossa. But this custom, dictated by both the division of property and social order, by no means implies that the poorer among the dead were slighted or despised. They too received signs of respect as far as the means available would allow. Corsican funeral rites were fundamentally extremely elaborate and of a highly dramatic character. The doors and shutters of the house afflicted by misfortune were closed, and sometimes the whole façade was painted black. The corpse, washed and freshly dressed, or in the not uncommon case of a violent death left in its bloodstained condition, was laid out in the parlour, which was usually less a room intended for the use of the living than the domain of dead members of the family, who were known as the *antichi* or *antinati*. This was where, after the introduction of photography, which in essence, after all, is nothing but a way of making ghostly apparitions materialize by means of a very dubious magical art, the living hung pictures of their parents, grandparents, and relations either close or more distant, who, although or even because they were no longer alive, were regarded as the true heads of the family. The wake was held beneath their uncompromising gaze, and on such occasions the women, otherwise condemned to silence, assumed the leading roles, singing laments and wailing all night, tearing their hair and scratching their faces like the Furies of old, particularly when the body was that of a murdered man; and to all appearances were quite beside themselves with blind rage and pain, while the men stood out in the dark entrance to the house or on the steps, pounding the floor with their rifle butts. Stephen Wilson points out that eyewitnesses present at such wakes in the nineteenth century, and up to the inter-war period, thought it remarkable that while the wailing women worked themselves up into a trance-like state, were overcome by dizziness and fainted away, they gave no impression at all of being overwhelmed by genuine emotion. Many accounts, says Wilson, even speak of a striking lack of feeling or rigidity in which the singer sheds not a single tear, even though her voice breaks convulsively with passion in the highest registers. In view of such apparently icy self-control, some commentators have been inclined to regard the laments of the *voceratrici* as a hollow sham, a spectacle prescribed by tradition, and this idea is supported by the observation that merely getting a chorus of mourners together will have called for a considerable amount of practical organization in advance and rational direction of the singing itself. In truth, of course, there is no discrepancy between such calculation and a genuine grief which actually makes the mourners seem beside themselves, for fluctuation between the expression of deeply felt sorrow, which can sound like a choking fit, and the aesthetically – even cunningly – modulated manipulation of the audience to whom that grief is displayed, has perhaps been the most typical characteristic of our severely disturbed species at every stage of civilization. Anthropological literature contains many descriptions by writers such as Frazer, Huizinga, Eliade, Lévi-Strauss and Rudolf Bilz of the members of early tribal cultures who, while celebrating their rites of initiation or sacrifice, retained a very precise and ever-present subliminal awareness that the compulsive extremes to which they went, always connected with the infliction of injury and mutilation, were in essence mere play-acting, even though the performance could sometimes approach the point of death. Those in severe psychological conditions also have a clear idea somewhere, in their inmost hearts, that they are literally acting body and soul in a play. Moreover, the pathological state of mind of the Corsican *voceratrici*, characterized by both total collapse and the utmost self-control, was probably not fundamentally different from that of the somnambulists who have fallen into carefully rehearsed paroxysms of hysteria on the stages of opera houses evening after evening for two hundred years or more. But in any case the lamentations in the dead person's darkened house, illuminated only by the flickering light of a single candle, were followed by the funeral feast. The expense to which the bereaved had to go for the sake of their own and the dead man's honour in this feast, which often lasted several days, was so great that it could ruin a family if bad luck brought several murders or fatal attacks in quick succession, perhaps as part of a blood feud. Mourning was worn for five years or longer; on her husband's death a widow stayed in mourning for the rest of her life. It is not surprising that the high-necked black dress and black headscarf, or the black corduroy suit, seemed to be Corsican national costume until well into the twentieth century. According to the accounts of earlier travellers, there was an aura of melancholy about those black figures seen everywhere in the streets of villages and towns and out in the country, an aura that even on the brightest sunlit days lay like a shadow over the green and leafy world of the island, and was reminiscent of the pictures of Poussin, for instance those depicting the Massacre of the Innocents or the death of Germanicus. Remembrance of the dead never really came to an end. Every year on All Souls' Day a table was especially laid for them in Corsican houses, or at least a few cakes were put out on the windowsill as if for hungry birds in winter, since it was thought that they visited in the middle of the night to take a morsel of food. And a tub of cooked chestnuts was left outside the door for the vagabond beggars who, in the minds of the settled population, represented restless wandering spirits. Since the dead are known to be always cold, people took care not to let the fire on the hearth go out before day dawned. All this indicates both the lasting grief of the bereaved and the fear they could barely assuage, for the dead were thought of as extremely touchy, envious, vengeful, quarrelsome and cunning. Given the least excuse, they would infallibly take their displeasure out on you. They were not regarded as beings for ever at a safe distance in the world beyond the grave, but as family members still present, although in a different condition, and forming a kind of solidarity in the *communità dei defunti* against those who were not yet dead. About a foot shorter than they had been in life, they went around in bands and groups, or sometimes followed a banner along the road, drawn up in regiments. They were heard talking and whispering in their strange piping voices, but nothing they said to each other could be understood except for the name of whoever they intended to come for next. There are many stories of their appearances and the methods they used to announce their presence. Until the very recent past there were people living who had seen pale lights above a house in which someone was soon to die, who heard a dog howling at the wrong time, or the squealing of a cart that stopped outside the gate after midnight, or the beat of drums from the darkness of the maquis. There, in that vast space still almost untouched by human hand, was the abode of the armies of the dead, and clad in the full, billowing cloaks of the brotherhood of corpses, or the colourful uniforms of fusiliers who had fallen on the battlefields of Wagram and Waterloo, they set out from the maquis to ensure that they received the share of life due to them. They were known from time immemorial as the *cumpagnia*, the *mumma* or the *squadra d'Arozza*, and they were believed to be bent on entering their former dwellings or even the churches, to say a blasphemous rosary as they prayed for a new recruit. And the power of the squadrons of the dead, increasing in numbers and strength year by year, was not all that must be feared: there were also individual restless ghosts intent on revenge, lying in wait by the roadside for travellers, suddenly emerging from behind a rock or manifesting themselves on the road itself, usually during the sinister hours of the day – at noon, when everyone was usually at table, or after the angelus was rung, when pale shadows discoloured the earth in the brief space of time between sunset and nightfall. And a man might often happen to return from working in the fields with the eerie news that in the middle of the empty countryside, where you usually knew everyone in your own or the next village by his bearing and his gait, he had seen a crook-backed stranger, if not the *fulcina* in person, the Reaper with sickle in hand. Dorothy Carrington, who frequently visited Corsica in the fifties and spent long periods there, says that a certain Jean Cesari, whom she had met in London and regarded as an enlightened man perfectly familiar with the principles of scientific thinking, and who later introduced her to the mysteries of his native Corsica, was firmly convinced of the real presence of ghosts, and indeed swore by his eyesight that he had seen and heard them himself. When he was asked in what form the ghosts appeared, and if you might meet dead friends and relations among them, Cesari said that at first glance they seemed to be like normal people, but as soon as you looked more closely their faces blurred and flickered at the edges, just like the faces of actors in an old movie. And sometimes only their upper bodies were clearly outlined, while the rest of them resembled drifting smoke. Over and beyond such stories, which are also handed down in other

31

popular cultures, there was still a widespread belief in Corsica, until well into the decades after the last war, that some special people were in a way in the service of death. These *culpa morti, acciatori* or *mazzeri*, as they were called, men as well as women, who were reliably said to come from every class of the population and outwardly differed not at all from other members of the community, were believed to have the ability to leave their bodies at home by night and go out hunting. Obeying a compulsion that came over them like a sickness, they were said to crouch in the darkness by rivers and springs, ready to strangle some creature, a fox or a hare, when it came to quench its thirst, and in the animal's distorted countenance such people, victims of this murderous form of noctambulism, would recognize the image of some inhabitant of their village, sometimes even a close relation, who from that terrible moment on was doomed to die. What lies behind this extremely bizarre superstition, something that we can hardly imagine today and which is obviously entirely untouched by Christian doctrine, is the awareness, arising from the family's shared suffering of an endless series of the most painful experiences, of a shadow realm extending into the light of day, a place where, in an act of perverse violence, the fate we shall finally meet is predetermined. But the people whom Dorothy Carrington called dream-hunters, the *acciatori*, now almost extinct, were not just the spawn of an imagination ruled by profound fatalism; they could also be cited as evidence for Freud's psychological theory – as enlightening as it is impossible to prove – that to the unconscious mind even those who die a natural death are victims of murder. I remember very well how, as a child, I stood for the first time by an open coffin, with the dull sense in my breast that my grandfather, lying there on wood shavings, had suffered a shameful injustice that none of us survivors could make good. And for some time, too, I have known that the more one has to bear, for whatever reason, of the burden of grief which is probably not imposed on the human species for nothing, the more often do we meet ghosts. On the Graben in Vienna, in the London Underground, at a reception given by the Mexican ambassador, at a lock-keeper's cottage on the Ludwigskanal in Bamberg, now here and now there, without expecting it, you may meet one of those beings who are somehow blurred and out of place and who, as I always feel, are a little too small and short-sighted; they have something curiously watchful about them, as if they were lying in wait, and their faces bear the expression of a race that wishes us ill. Not long ago, when I was queuing at the supermarket checkout, a very dark-skinned man, almost pitch-black in colour, stood in front of me with a large and, as it turned out, entirely empty suitcase into which, after paying for them, he put the Nescafé, the biscuits and the few other things he had bought. He had probably arrived in Norwich only yesterday from Zaire or Uganda to study, I thought, and then forgot him, until towards evening of the same day the three daughters of one of our neighbours knocked on our door bringing the news that their father had died before dawn of a severe heart attack. They are still around us, the dead, but there are times when I think that perhaps they will soon be gone. Now that we have reached a point where the number of those alive on earth has doubled within just three decades, and will treble within the next generation, we need no longer fear the once overwhelming numbers of the dead. Their significance is visibly decreasing. We can no longer speak of everlasting memory and the veneration of our forebears. On the contrary: the dead must now be cleared out of the way as quickly and comprehensively as possible. What mourner at a crematorium funeral has not thought, as the coffin moves into the furnace, that the way we now take leave of the dead is marked by ill-concealed and paltry haste? And the room allotted to them becomes smaller and smaller; they are often given notice to leave after only a few years. Where will their mortal remains go then, how will they be disposed of? It is a fact that there is great pressure on space, even here in the country. What must it be like in the cities inexorably moving towards the thirty million mark? Where will they all go, the dead of

Buenos Aires and São Paulo, of Mexico City, Lagos and Cairo, Tokyo, Shanghai and Bombay? Very few of them, probably, into a cool grave. And who has remembered them, who remembers them at all? To remember, to retain and to preserve, Pierre Bertaux wrote of the mutation of mankind even thirty years ago, was vitally important only when population density was low, we manufactured few items, and nothing but space was present in abundance. You could not do without anyone then, even after death. In the urban societies of the late twentieth century, on the other hand, where everyone is instantly replaceable and is really superfluous from birth, we have to keep throwing ballast overboard, forgetting everything that we might otherwise remember: youth, childhood, our origins, our forebears and ancestors. For a while the site called the Memorial Grove recently set up on the Internet may endure; here you can lay those particularly close to you to rest electronically and visit them. But this virtual cemetery too will dissolve into the ether, and the whole past will flow into a formless, indistinct, silent mass. And leaving a present without memory, in the face of a future that no individual mind can now envisage, in the end we shall ourselves relinquish life without feeling any need to linger at least for a while, nor shall we be impelled to pay return visits from time to time.

The Alps in the Sea

Once upon a time Corsica was entirely covered by forest. Storey by storey it grew for thousands of years in rivalry with itself, up to heights of fifty metres and more, and who knows, perhaps larger and larger species would have evolved, trees reaching to the sky, if the first settlers had not appeared and if, with the typical fear felt by their own kind for its place of origin, they had not steadily forced the forest back again.

The degradation of the most highly developed plant species is a process known to have begun near what we call the cradle of civilization. Most of the high forests that once grew all the way to the Dalmatian, Iberian and North African coasts had already been cut down by the beginning of the present era. Only in the interior of Corsica did a few forests of trees towering far taller than those of today remain, and they were still being described with awe by nineteenth-century travellers, although now they have almost entirely disappeared. Of the silver firs that were among the dominant tree species of Corsica in the Middle Ages, standing everywhere in the mists clinging to the mountains, on overshadowed slopes and in ravines, only a few relics are now left in the Marmano valley and the Forêt de Puntiello, and on a walk there a remembered image came into my mind of a forest in the Innerfern through which I had once gone as a child with my grandfather.

A history of the forests of France by Etienne de la Tour, published during the Second Empire, speaks of individual firs growing to a height of almost sixty metres during their lives of over a thousand years, and they, so de la Tour writes, are the last trees to convey some idea of the former grandeur of the European forests. He laments the destruction of the Corsican forests *'par des exploitations mal conduites'* ('by mismanaged exploitation'), which was already becoming a clear menace in his time. The stands of trees spared longest were those in the most inaccessible regions, for instance the great forest of Bavella, which covered the Corsican Dolomites between Sartène and Solenzara and was largely untouched until towards the end of the nineteenth century.

The English landscape painter and writer Edward Lear, who travelled in Corsica in the summer of 1876, wrote of the immense forests that then rose high from the blue twilight of the Solenzara valley and clambered up the steepest slopes, all the way to the vertical cliffs and precipices with their overhangs, cornices and upper terraces where smaller groups of trees stood like plumes on a helmet. On the more level surfaces at the head of the pass, the soft ground on which you walked was densely overgrown with all kinds of different bushes and herbs. Arbutus grew here, a great many ferns, heathers and juniper bushes, grasses, asphodels and dwarf cyclamen, and from all these low-growing plants rose the grey trunks of Laricio pines, their green parasols seeming to float free far, far above in the crystal-clear air.

'At three the top of the pass . . . is reached,' says Lear, 'and here the real forest of Bavella commences, lying in a deep cup-like hollow between this and the opposite ridge, the north and south side of the valley being formed by the tremendous columns and peaks of granite . . . which stood up like two gigantic portions of a vast amphitheatre', with the sea beyond them, and the Italian coast like a brush-stroke drawn on paper. These crags, he writes, 'are doubly awful and magnificent now that one is close to them, and excepting the heights of Serbal and Sinai, they exceed in grandeur anything of the kind I have ever seen'. But Lear also comments on the timber carts drawn by fourteen or sixteen mules which even then were making their way along the sharply winding road, transporting single trunks a hundred to a hundred and twenty feet long and up to six feet in diameter, an observation that I found confirmed in 1879 by the *Dictionnaire de Géographie* edited by Vivien de Saint Martin, in which the Dutch traveller and topographer Melchior van de Velde writes that he has never seen a finer forest than the forest of Bavella, not even in Switzerland, Lebanon or on the islands of Indochina. *'Bavella est ce que j'ai vu de plus beau en fait de forêts,'* says van de Velde, adding this warning: *'Seulement, si le touriste veut la voir dans sa gloire, qu'il se hâte! La hache s'y promène et Bavella s'en va!'* ('Of the forests I have seen, Bavella is the loveliest . . . Only, if the tourist wishes to see it in its glory, he must make haste! The axe is abroad and Bavella is disappearing!') And indeed, nothing in the Bavella area today is as it must then have been. It is true that when you first climb to the pass from the south, coming closer and closer to the rocky peaks, which are violet to purple in colour and are often surrounded halfway up by wreaths of vapour, and then look down from the edge of the Bocca into the Solenzara valley, it seems at first as if the wonderful forests praised by van de Velde and Lear were still standing. In truth, however, no trees grow here except those planted by the forestry department on the site of the great fire of the summer of 1960: slender conifers which cannot be imagined lasting a single human lifetime, let alone for dozens of generations.

The ground under these meagre pines is largely bare: I myself saw not the slightest trace of the wealth of game mentioned by earlier travellers – 'le gibier y abonde,' writes van de Velde. Ibex were once extremely abundant here, eagles and vultures soared above the rock-slides, hundreds of siskins and finches darted through the canopy of the forest, quail and partridge nested under the low shrubs, and butterflies fluttered everywhere around. The creatures of Corsica are said to have been strikingly small in size, a phenomenon which sometimes occurs on islands.

Ferdinand Gregorovius, who travelled in Corsica in 1852, mentions an entomologist from Dresden whom he met in the hills above Sartène, and who told him that the island had struck him as a paradise garden on his first visit, particularly because of the small size of its fauna species, and indeed, writes Gregorovius, soon after he met the Saxon entomologist he had several sightings in the forest of Bavella of the Tyrrhenian red deer *Cervus elaphus corsicanus*, now long since extinct, an animal of dwarfish stature and almost oriental appearance, with a head much too large for the rest of its body, and eyes wide with fear in constant expectation of death.

Although the game that once lived in such abundance in the forests of the island has been eradicated almost without trace today, the fever of the chase still breaks out on Corsica every September. During my excursions into the interior of the island I repeatedly felt as if the entire male population were participating in a ritual of destruction which long ago became pointless. The older men, usually wearing blue dungarees, are posted beside the road all the way up into the mountains; the young men, in a kind of paramilitary gear, drive around in jeeps and cross-country vehicles as if they thought the countryside were occupied, or they were expecting an enemy invasion. Unshaven, carrying heavy rifles, menacing in their manner, they look like those Croatian and Serbian militiamen who destroyed their native land in their deranged belligerence, and like those Marlboro-style heroes of the Yugoslavian civil war, the Corsican hunters are not to be trifled with if you happen to stray into their territory.

More than once on such meetings they plainly indicated that they did not want to talk to some chance-come hiker about their sanguinary business, and sent me on my way with a gesture making it clear that anyone who did not get out of the danger zone very quickly might easily be shot down. Once, a little way below Evisa, I tried to strike up a conversation with one of the hunters posted beside the road and obviously taking his task very seriously, a short man of around sixty who was sitting, his double-barrelled shotgun across his knees, on the low stone balustrade which fences off the road at that point from the ravine of the Gorges de Spelunca, where it drops to two hundred metres below. The cartridges he had with him were very large, and the belt carrying them was so broad that it reached like a leather jerkin from his belly to halfway up his chest. When I asked him what he was looking for he simply replied *'Sangliers'* ('Wild boars'), as if that alone must suffice to send me packing. He would not have his photograph taken, but warded me off with his outspread hand just as guerrillas do in front of the camera.

In the Corsican newspapers, the so-called *ouverture de la chasse* (the start of the hunting season) is one of the main subjects of reporting in September, together with the never-ending accounts of the bombing of police stations, local authority tax offices and other public institutions, and it even casts into the shade the excitement over the start of the new school year which seizes annually upon the entire French nation. Articles are published about the state of the game preserves in the various regions, last season's hunting, prospects for the present campaign, and indeed hunting in general in every imaginable form. And the papers print photographs of men of martial appearance emerging from the maquis with their guns over their shoulders, or posing around a dead boar. The main subject, however, is the lamentable fact that fewer and fewer hares and partridges can be found every year.

'*Mon mari,*' complains the wife of a hunter from

Vissavona to a *Corse-Matin* reporter, for instance, '*mon mari, qui rentrait toujours avec cinq ou six perdrix, on a tout juste pris une.*' ('My husband, who always used to come home with five or six partridges, got only one.') In a way the contempt she expresses for the husband coming home empty-handed from his foray into the wilderness, the indisputably ludicrous appearance of the ultimately unsuccessful hunter in the eyes of his wife, women always having been excluded from the hunt, is the closing episode of a story that looks far back into our dark past, and one which even in my childhood filled me with uneasy premonitions.

I remember, for instance, how on my way to school I once passed Wohlfahrt the butcher's yard on a frosty autumn morning, just as a dozen deer were being un-loaded from a cart and tipped out on the paving stones. I could not move from the spot for a long time, so spellbound was I by the sight of the dead animals. Even then the fuss made by the hunters about sprigs of fir, and the palms arranged in the butcher's empty white-tiled shop window on Sundays, seemed to me somehow dubious. Bakers obviously needed no such decorations.

Later, in England, I saw rows of little green plastic trees hardly an inch high surrounding cuts of meat and offal displayed in the shop windows of 'Family Butchers'. The obvious fact that these evergreen plastic ornaments must be mass-produced somewhere for the sole purpose

43

of alleviating our sense of guilt about the bloodshed seemed to me, in its very absurdity, to show how strongly we desire absolution and how cheap we have always bought it.

All this was going through my head again one afternoon as I sat at the window of my hotel room in Piana. I had found an old volume of the *Bibliothèque de la Pléiade* in the drawer of the bedside table, and I began to read Flaubert's version of the legend of St Julian, which I had not known before, that strange tale in which an insatiable passion for hunting and a vocation for sainthood do battle in the same heart. I was both fascinated and disturbed by the story, which in itself I approached with reluctance.

Even the episode of the killing of the church mouse, an explosion of violence in a boy who until that moment had always behaved well, got under my skin most uncomfortably. We are told that Julian, waiting by the mousehole, gave the creature a small tap and was taken aback to see that its little body had stopped moving. A drop of blood stained the flagstones. And the longer the story went on, the more blood there was. Time after time, the crime must be masked by another kind of death. The pigeon brought down by Julian with his sling lies twitching in a privet bush, and as he wrings its neck he feels his senses faint with pleasure. As soon as he has learned the art of the chase from his father the urge comes over him to go out into the wilderness. Now he is forever hunting wild boar in the forest, bear in the mountains, deer in the valleys or out in open country. The animals take fright at the sound of the drum, hounds race over the hillsides, hawks rise in the air and birds drop like stones from the sky.

The huntsman comes home every evening covered with mud and blood, and so the killing goes on and on until, one icy cold winter's morning, Julian goes out and, in a day-long frenzy, strikes down everything moving around him. Arrows fall, we are told, like rain beating down in a thunderstorm. In the end night comes, the sunset is red among the branches of the forest like a cloth soaked with blood, and Julian leans against a tree with his eyes wide open, looking at the vast extent of the slaughter and wondering how he can have done it. He then falls victim to a paralysis of the soul, and begins his long wanderings through a world which is no longer in a state of grace, sometimes in such blazing heat that the hair on his head catches fire of its own accord in the glow of the sun, at other times in cold so icy that it breaks his limbs. He refuses to hunt any more, but sometimes his terrible passion comes over him again in his dreams; he sees himself, like our father Adam, surrounded by all the creatures in the garden of paradise, and he has only to reach out his arm and they are dead. Or he sees them passing by in pairs before his eyes, beginning with aurochs and elephant and going on all the way to the peacocks, guineafowl and ermines as they looked on the day they entered the Ark. From the darkness of a cave he hurls darts that never miss their mark, yet more and more follow without end.

Wherever he goes, wherever he turns, the ghosts of the animals he has killed are with him, until at last, after much hardship and suffering, he is rowed by a leper across the water to the end of the world. On the opposite bank Julian must share the ferryman's bed, and then, as he embraces the man's fissured and ulcerated flesh, partly hard and gnarled, partly deliquescent, spending the night breast to breast and mouth to mouth with that most repellent of all human beings, he is released from his torment and may rise into the blue expanses of the firmament.

Not once as I read could I take my eyes off this utterly perverse tale of the despicable nature of human violence, a story that probes horror further with every line. Only the act of grace when the saint is transfigured on the last page let me look up again.

Evening twilight was already darkening half of my room. Outside, however, the setting sun still hung above the sea, and in the blazing light that rippled from it the whole of that section of world visible from my window quivered, a view unspoilt by the line of any road or the smallest human settlement. The monstrous rock formations of Les Calanques, carved from granite over millions of years by wind, salt mist and rain, and towering up 300 metres from the depths, shone in fiery copper red as if the stone itself were in flames, glowing from within. Sometimes I thought I saw the outlines of plants and animals burning in that flickering light, or the shapes of a whole race of people stacked into a great pyre. Even the water below seemed to be aflame.

Only as the sun sank beneath the horizon was the surface of the sea extinguished; the fire in the rocks faded, turned lilac and blue, and shadows moved out from the coast. It took my eyes some time to become accustomed to the soft twilight, and then I could see the ship that had emerged from the middle of the fire and was now making for Porto harbour so slowly that you felt it was not moving at all. It was a white yacht with five masts, and left not the slightest wake on the still water. Although almost motionless, it moved forward as inexorably as the big hand of a clock. The ship was moving, so to speak, along the line dividing what we can perceive from what no one has ever yet seen.

Far out above the sea the last gleam of daylight faded; inland, the darkness was gathering closer and closer, until the lights on board the snow-white ship showed against the black heights of Capo Senino and the Scandola peninsula. Through my binoculars I saw the warm glow in the cabin windows, the lanterns on the superstructure of the deck, the sparkling garlands of light slung from mast to mast, but no other sign of life at all. For perhaps an hour the ship lay there at rest, shining in the dark, as if its captain were waiting for permission to put in to the harbour hidden behind Les Calanques. Then, as the stars began to show above the mountains, it turned and moved away again as slowly as it had come.

La cour de l'ancienne école

After this picture was sent to me last December, with a friendly request for me to think of something appropriate to say about it, it lay on my desk for some weeks, and the longer it lay there and the more often I looked at it the further it seemed to withdraw from me, until the task, in itself nothing worth mentioning, became an insuperable obstacle looming ahead. Then one day at the end of January, not a little to my relief, the picture suddenly disappeared from the place where it lay, and no one knew where it had gone. When some time had passed and I had almost entirely forgotten it, it unexpectedly returned, this time in a letter from Bonifacio in which Mme Séraphine Aquaviva, with whom I had been corresponding since the summer before, told me that she would be interested to know how I had come by the drawing enclosed without comment in my letter of 27 January, showing the yard of the old school of Porto Vecchio which she had attended in the thirties. At that time, Mme Aquaviva's letter continued, Porto Vecchio was a town almost dead, constantly plagued by malaria, surrounded by salt marshes, swamps and impenetrable green scrub. Once a month at most a rusty freighter came from Leghorn to take a load of oak planks aboard on the quayside. Otherwise nothing happened, except that everything went on rotting and decaying as it had for centuries. There was always a strange silence in the streets, since half the population were drowsing the day away indoors, shaking with fever, or sitting on steps and in doorways looking sallow and hollow-cheeked. We schoolchildren, said Mme Aquaviva, knowing nothing else, of course had no idea of the futility of our lives in a town made practically uninhabitable by paludism, as the phenomenon was called at the time. Like other children in more fortunate areas, we learned arithmetic and writing, and were taught various anecdotes about the rise and fall of the Emperor Napoleon. From time to time we looked out of the window, across the wall of the schoolyard and over the white rim of the lagoon, into the dazzling light that trembled far out over the Tyrrhenian Sea. Otherwise, Mme Aquaviva concluded her letter, I have almost no memories of my schooldays, except that whenever our teacher, a former hussar called Toussaint Benedetti, bent over my work he would say: *'Ce que tu écris mal,*

Séraphine! Comment veux-tu qu'on puisse te lire?' ('How badly you write, Séraphine! How do you expect anyone to read that?')

Essays

Strangeness, Integration and Crisis

On Peter Handke's play *Kaspar*

> *We must therefore listen attentively to every whisper of the world,*
> *trying to detect the images that have never made their way into*
> *poetry, the phantasms that have never reached a waking state. No*
> *doubt this is an impossible task in two senses: first because it would*
> *force us to reconstitute the dust of those actual sufferings and foolish*
> *words that nothing preserves in time; second, and above all, because*
> *those sufferings and words exist only in the act of separation.*
>
> Michel Foucault, *Madness and Civilization.*

When, after several panic-stricken attempts, Kaspar emerges on stage from behind the backdrop of a curtain, and at first does not move from the spot in that strange space, 'he is the incarnation of astonishment'.[1] At the end of what seems to us to have been a long flight he finds himself in a clearing, hemmed in without any way of escape, delivered up to a reality of which he has no concept. He knows nothing about us. It may be that in his colourful jacket, wide trousers and hat with its band he reminds us of the wide-eyed rustics who used to make Viennese audiences laugh. As wily provincials these rustics of course knew their way around, not perhaps in urban society *comme il faut* but on stage, where they were never at a loss for either information or an excuse. But Kaspar is still a stranger here and has no companions. The theme of the play, then, is not the fast-moving adventures of the comic character, which are happily resolved in the end, but the inner and inward-looking story of the taming of a wild human being. The result, however, is to cast a critical light on what the development of the outer plot constantly implies in its specific and historical course: the transformation of the unruly clowning into a proper Kasperl* play, the attempt, in many ways a hopeless one, to turn an individual who by ordinary standards is uncivilized into a respectable citizen.

We have to make do with conjectures about Kaspar's previous life. The novel by Jakob Wassermann tells us that 'no one knew where he hailed from', and that he himself, being incapable of language, could give no information about his origins.[2] However, his unheralded, defenceless presence signifies the living provocation of social resentment. We suspect that the speechless creature, as yet entirely untaught, is in possession of a secret of his own, if not actually in a state of paradisal bliss.

*The 'Kasperl' play is the German version of a Punch and Judy show.

And that, says Nietzsche, perspicacious in such matters, 'is hard on a man. He may ask the animal: ''Why do you just look at me instead of telling me about your happiness?'' The animal wants to reply: ''Because I always immediately forget what I wanted to say'' – but then it forgets even this answer and says nothing.'³ It is rather like that with Kaspar and his prompters in the play. They envy him the blankness of the life he represents, his ability – to quote Nietzsche again – to be 'totally unhistorical'.⁴ At the same time this special quality is the reason for Kaspar's strangeness. Hofmannsthal has linked similar conjectures with his concept of pre-existence, a state of painlessness beyond trauma in which a barely perceptible happiness, which is mere and simple existence, persists uninterrupted. Wassermann's novel too tries to present this state as something very different from the deprivation of imprisonment. 'He did not sense any changes in his own physical condition,' says Wassermann of Hauser, 'or wish for anything to be different.'⁵ Kaspar's placid existence is illustrated in the symbol of a 'white wooden horse . . . that mirrored his own existence darkly . . . He did not talk to it, not even in silent imagined exchanges, and although it stood on a board that had wheels it never occurred to him to push it to and fro.'⁶ From such a static existence, a life without a history in which one might acquire the art of hearing 'wood rotting over long distances' and in which 'Caspar could make out colours even in the dark', he is released into the light of the stage, a shocking and painful transition to surroundings that are qualitatively entirely new, where the 'originally prestabilized harmony' is lost, and his inner resources prove inadequate.[7] Anthropological theory assumes that exposure in a treeless situation where all escape upwards was cut off led to the invention of myths. Kafka's ape, dragged into human society, expresses very similar ideas in his 'Report for an Academy'. It is the absence of any way of escape that has forced him to become human himself. 'I had always had so many ways out, you see, and now I have none.'[8] So the wild boy Kaspar has no choice but to develop, except that in his case, as in the ape Rotpeter's, the myth does not have to be invented: it is provided for him by his professional prompters. Their disembodied voices have little to do with the optimistic educational theories of the eighteenth century and later, according to which it might be hoped that Kaspar Hauser would educate himself to become a liberated, guiltless human being, a natural wonder. If such experiments showed naive idealism, the general approach to Kaspar resulted only in an illusion of liberation, entirely adapted to existing circumstances. An ego is formed until finally, as Hofmannsthal described it, it slips into another identity, 'like a dog, eerily silent and strange'.[9]

To Kaspar, the anonymous voices of the media to

which he is constantly exposed mean 'alienation in the sense of a passive submission to invasion by others'.[10] Something in him cracks; he becomes vulnerable and begins to learn. At first Kaspar's reactions to the refractory nature of the inanimate objects around him and his own incompetence as a human being are those of a clown. His hands get stuck down the side of the sofa, the table drawer falls out at his feet, he becomes entangled in a chair, a rocking chair tips over and Kaspar runs away, terrified, for every new lesson is a new horror to him. A clown merely performs an amusing act in the 'tension between the serious mastery of objects that has been learned and his own deliberate clumsiness',[11] but to the uneducated Kaspar such acts cannot be foreseen and relate not so much to the mastery of inanimate objects as to his own training. Handke has written, of the circus, that the audience's enthusiasm is never really free 'because the imminence of shame or horror is always present',[12] something could easily go wrong with the act. 'With a clown, however, the misfortune that is so embarrassing in all other circus numbers is planned as part of the act . . . His accidents are not awkward but comic. Indeed, it is an embarrassing sight if he does for once, unintentionally, *succeed* in mastering inanimate objects. The sight of a clown who fails to fall over a stool or who can sit down easily in an armchair . . . is embarrassing.'[13] Kaspar's clumsiness, however, is far from intentional, and the accidents he suffers are only very superficially comic. He soon learns to avoid them. But he has still assimilated enough clownish behaviour for us to be almost embarrassed by his correct reactions as the action continues. What looks like progress is really nothing but the gradual humiliation of a trained creature who, in approaching the human average, begins to resemble an animal gone mad. Kaspar's *éducation sentimentale* is also his case history, and from it we finally gain insight into the pathological connection which inevitably exists between the possession of property and education. For do not things have names only to help us to grasp them better, as if the blank spaces in the atlas we have made for ourselves out of reality disappear only so that the colonial empire of the mind may grow? 'As a child,' Henny Porten remembers during *Ritt über den Bodensee* ['The Ride Across Lake Constance'], 'if I wanted something, I always had to say what it was called first.'[14] Kaspar soon realizes that this is where the secret of mastering things lies; he becomes eager for information so that he will gain a little more power. Musil's claim that knowledge is related to greed and represents a despicable urge to hoard, as 'the fundamental and favourite expression of capitalism'[15] could be the critique of a development such as Kaspar's once he understands the point of learning. It is not that he makes a conscious choice between naivety and enlightenment, but the strange words that he uses in order to master strange things force themselves on him like commands and latent threats against which he cannot defend himself. Nor does he yet recognize the voices of society as something different, something outside him; instead, they echo within him as the part of himself that became strange to him when he was cast up in this new, over-bright environment. Social maxims and reflections overwhelm him as compulsively as if they were his own individual delusion. Consequently, he obeys them.

The merciless education of Kaspar obeys the laws of language. The reason why the play could be described, says Handke, as 'speech torture' is not just that other people talk to Kaspar until he loses what might be called his sound animal reason. More precisely, in this learning process speech itself features as an arsenal containing a cruel set of instruments. Kaspar's very first sentence helps him, as the prompters explain, 'learn to divide time into time before and time after uttering of the sentence'.[16] Tension arises, and with it a foretaste of the torture. Kaspar learns to hesitate as he speaks, and the voices show him how that hesitation can make painful incisions where they do not belong, separating the parts of a sentence: 'The sentence doesn't hurt you yet, not one word. Does hurt you. Every word does. Hurt, but you don't know that that which hurts you is a sentence that. Sentence hurts you because you don't know that it is a sentence.'[17] What the prompters demonstrate through speech can be transferred, becomes an act of incision, the vivisection of reality and ultimately of a human being. Within it the diffuse pain of being unaware becomes the keen torment of experience. In the obsessive attempt to find a reason for the animation of life, a world of images is divided into its anatomical components. This is the nature of speech operating successfully. Its grammar can be perceived as a mechanical system that gradually carves the crucial terms on the skin of the torture victim, and the torture arises from the combination of its apparatus with the organism. Kafka described the prerequisites for this process in his story 'In the Penal Colony', and Nietzsche, in discussing mnemonic techniques in the *Genealogy of Morals*, thought there was nothing more sinister in the prehistory of mankind than the combination of pain and recollection to construct a memory. But what is taken from the living substance of the individual in the long process of his training to become an articulate, moral human being adheres to the linguistic machine until in the end the parts become interchangeable in function. Lars Gustafsson, who designed an image of the grammatical machine, wonders whether the symbolical value of machinery does not perhaps lie in the fact 'that it reminds us of the possibility that our own lives could be something simulated, in a sense resembling the life of machines themselves'.[18] A human being, then, is a Stymphalian creature of metal screws and springs, stamping accepted patterns out of the metal of communication, and speech is an apparatus run out of control and beginning to lead a sinister life of its own. Model sentences such as those suggested to Kaspar are reflexes of the cruel treatment to which his sensory apparatus is submitted by its linguistic shaping. 'The door springs open. The skin springs open. The match burns. The slap burns. The grass trembles. The fearful girl trembles. The slap in the face smacks. The body smacks. The tongue licks. The flame licks. The saw screeches. The torture victim screeches. The lark trills. The policeman trills. The blood stops. The breath stops.'[19] The prompters know this too. At the beginning of the second part, when the injured Kaspar has split by simple division into two contented entities, the prompters utter an apologia for the process that initiates the candidate into a society where everything is regular. 'Intermittent smashing / of a stick / on your jug / is no balm / nor a reason / to bewail the lack of law and order / this season / a sip of lye / in your mug / or a prick / in the guts / or a stick / in the nuts / being wriggled about / or something of that order / only pricklier / fearlessly / introduced in the ears / so as to / get someone hopping / and pop in order / by all means / at your command / but chiefly / without being / overly / fussy / over the means – / that / is no reason / to lose any words / over the lack of order.'[20]

Kaspar is thus systematically socialized. He makes visible progress. But then suddenly he finds himself in crisis. His identity is undermined by the passing of time. 'When I am, I was.'[21] He formulates this problem of shifting phases in the most confusing variations, constantly mixing up the grammatically possible and the grammatically impossible, his reality and his irritation constantly becoming confused. When he finally says, 'I will have become because I am',[22] we can no longer tell if he has it the wrong way round or is simply expressing hopelessness. Kaspar, now uncertain of himself, three times repeats the magical formula, 'I am the one I am.' But the affirmation sounds wide of the mark. In its abstraction it does not offer anything sufficient to counter Kaspar's growing doubt of what he represents. As if in alarm he stops rocking and cries, 'Why are there so many black worms flying about?' It is an image of the utmost distress. Kaspar is in danger of regression. The stage darkens, and once more the prompters must try persuasion. It grows light again, and they begin to speak. 'You have model sentences with which you can get through life.' The light grows brighter. 'You can learn and make yourself useful.'[23] And the brighter it becomes, the quieter Kaspar is; he is all right again, enlightened, ready for the shock of confirmation, for the test of a total blackout, in which a prompter tells him, 'You've been cracked open.'[24] This time the darkness of the stage is not a fear that Kaspar already has but one that is instilled into him. Only after a long moment does a voice suggest, in the darkness, 'You become sensitive to dirt.' When it is light again, Kaspar's socialization finally seems complete. His alter ego enters with a broom, sweeping the stage. Kaspar is now his own matrix, with unlimited powers of reproduction. More Kaspars appear, clones of his reformed person. But now Kaspar will begin to suffer from this fact, from everything that is repeated, and thus not least from himself. 'I was proud of the first step I took, of the second step I felt ashamed: I felt ashamed of everything that I repeated.'[25] Only with speech was it the other way round, for, says Kaspar, 'I felt ashamed even of the first sentence I uttered, whereas I no longer felt ashamed of the second sentence.' Speech, as it were, had removed his shame, teaching him to become accustomed to identities. The fact that he still remembers it is the beginning of the story he tells of himself towards the end of the play. This story is the clear signal that all is not yet right with him, for 'an object is orderly when you don't first have to tell a story about it'.[26] Kaspar's education thus seems to have failed. He remembers, but too well. He knows not only about himself but about his origin and development, about his indoctrination, the prelude to his despair.

In reflecting on the changes that have happened to him, Kaspar breaks out of the role that he was given to play. His inquiries take him back to a point when, entering paradise through the gateway of thought, he regains the naivety of his pre-existence. He remembers uttering his first sentence, and in the nostalgia of such memories he encounters the unconscious perfection of his lost self. 'Then once I took a look into the open, where there was a very green glow, and I said to the open: I want to be someone like somebody else was once? – and with this sentence I wanted to ask the open why it was that my feet were aching.'[27] Sinking into such reminiscences he gauges time, seeks the darkness of his life which is now almost stripped of any mystery, until he comes upon things that are identical with his own reality, not just the reality he has assimilated. He remembers the snow that stung his hand, the landscape that 'at that time was a brightly coloured window shutter', and was then like a colourful shop window, and a gloomy legacy of 'candles and bloodsuckers; ice and mosquitoes; horses and pus; hoarfrost and rats; eels and sicklebills'.[28] These images, retrieved and re-created from his pre-existence, images in which Kaspar's earlier life shows a relationship with Sigismund's in Hofmannsthal's *Der Turm*, seem to him like authentic documents of his being. Thanks to them he can say, 'I still experienced myself.' The training to which he has been subjected could not entirely obliterate his memory of his beginnings. He can still go back behind what he has learned. The wild metaphors he brings back from such excursions are, in their disparate nature, like what have been called the 'metaphors of a paranoia . . . a poetic protest against the invasion of others'.[29] The crystallization point of this sign of intended rejection comes at those moments when, as Handke says in *Wunschloses Unglück* ['A Sorrow Beyond Dreams'] 'the utmost need to communicate comes together with the ultimate speechlessness'.[30] However, where images escape that paralytic confrontation they feature, being impenetrable ciphers, as examples of broken rebellion. Their structure is that of the myth in which fact and fiction are, so to speak, inseparably linked together. And like that myth, they 'involve the same sort of outrageous distortion . . . all symbolism harbours the curse of mediacy; it is bound to obscure what it seeks to reveal. Thus the sound of speech strives to ''express'' subjective and objective happening, the ''inner'' and the ''outer'' world; but what of this it can retain is not the life and individual fullness of existence, but only a dead abbreviation of it.'[31] Literature can transcend this dilemma only by keeping faith with unsocial, banned language, and by learning to use the opaque images of broken rebellion as a means of communication.

Between History and Natural History

On the literary description of total destruction

The trick of elimination is every expert's defensive reflex.

Stanislaw Lem, *Imaginary Magnitude*

I drove through ruined Cologne late at dusk, with terror of the world and of men and of myself in my heart.

Victor Gollancz, *In Darkest Germany*

To this day there is no adequate explanation of why the destruction of the German cities towards the end of the Second World War was not (with those few exceptions that prove the rule) taken as a subject for literary depiction either then or later, although significant conclusions could certainly have been drawn from this admittedly complex problem. It might, after all, have been supposed that the air raids very methodically carried out over the years and directly affecting large sections of the population of Germany, as well as the radical social changes resulting from the destruction, would have been an incitement to writers to set down something about such experiences. The dearth of literary records from which anything might be learned of the extent and consequences of the destruction which is so obvious to a later generation, although those involved clearly felt no need to commemorate it, is all the more remarkable because accounts of the development of West German literature frequently speak of what they call *Trümmer-literatur* (the literature of the ruins). Heinrich Böll, for instance, says of that genre in a book written in 1952: 'And so we write of the war, of homecoming, of what we had seen in the war and what we found on returning home: we write of ruins.'[1] The same author's *Frankfurter Vorlesungen* ['Frankfurt Lectures'] contains the comment: 'Where would 1945, that historic moment in time, be without Eich and Celan, Borchert and Nossack, Kreuder, Aichinger and Schnurre, Richter, Kolbenhoff, Schroers, Langgässer, Krolow, Lenz, Schmidt, Andersch, Jens and Marie Luise von Kaschnitz?[2] The Germany of the years 1945–1954 would have vanished long ago had it not found expression in the literature of the time.'[3] One may feel a certain sympathy for such statements, but they hardly offset the near-incontrovertible fact that the literature cited here, which is sufficiently known to have dealt primarily with 'personal matters' and the private feelings of its protagonists, is of relatively slight value as a source of information on the objective reality of the time, more particularly the devastation of the German cities and the patterns of psychological and social behaviour affected by it. It is remarkable, to say the least, that up to Alexander Kluge's account of the air raid of 8 April 1945 on Halberstadt, published in 1977 as Number 2 in his series of *Neue Geschichten* ['New Stories'], there was no literary work that to any degree filled up this lacuna in German memory, which is surely more than coincidental, and that Hans Erich Nossack and Hermann Kasack, the only writers who attempted any literary account of the new historical factor of total destruction, embarked upon their works in that vein while the war was still in progress, and sometimes even anticipated actual events. In his reminiscences of Hermann Kasack, Nossack writes:

At the end of 1942 or the beginning of 1943 I sent him thirty pages of a prose work which after the end of the war was to become my story *Nekyia*. Thereupon Kasack challenged me to a competition in prose. I didn't understand what he meant by that; only much later did it become clear to me. We were both dealing with the same subject at the time, the destroyed or dead city. Today it may seem that it was not too difficult to foresee the destruction of our cities. But it is still remarkable that before the event two writers were trying to take an objective view of the totally unreal kind of reality in which we had to spend years at the time, and in which we fundamentally still find ourselves, accepting it as the form of existence allotted to us.[4]

The way that literature reacted to the collective experience of the destruction of whole tracts of human life and – as some of Nossack's writings anticipating the documentary style show – the way it *could* have reacted will be illustrated here by Kasack's novel *Die Stadt hinter dem Strom* ['The City Beyond the River'] and Nossack's 'Der Untergang' ['The End'], which was written in the summer of 1943.

Kasack's novel, published in 1947 and one of the first 'successes' of post-war German literature,[5] had almost no effect on the literary strategies which were formed against the background of political and social restoration in the late 1940s. The reason was probably that the book's aesthetic and moral aims largely corresponded to the ideas developed by the so-called 'internal emigrants',* and thus to the style of that time, which was already obsolescent in the year of the novel's publication. The determining feature of Kasack's work is the contradiction it presents between the utter hopelessness of the present situation and an attempt to subject the remnants of a humanist view of the world to a new if negative synthesis. In its concrete details the topography of the city beyond the river, in which 'life, so to speak, is lived underground',[6] is the topography of destruction. 'Only

* 'Internal emigrants' were those people who, while dissociating themselves intellectually from the Nazi regime, remained in Germany during the Hitler period.

the façades of the buildings in the surrounding streets still stood, so that a sideways glance through the rows of empty windows gave a view of the sky.'[7] And it could be argued that the account of the 'lifeless life'[8] of the people in the limbo of this twilight kingdom was also inspired by the real economic and social situation between 1943 and 1947. There are no vehicles anywhere, and pedestrians walk the ruined streets apathetically, 'as if they no longer felt the bleak nature of their surroundings'.[9] Others 'could be seen in the ruined dwellings, now deprived of their purpose, searching for buried remnants of household goods, here salvaging a bit of tin or wire from the rubble, there picking up a few splinters of wood and stowing them in the bags they wore slung around them, which resembled botanical specimen tins'.[10] There is a sparse assortment of junk for sale in the roofless shops: 'Here a few jackets and trousers, belts with silver buckles, ties and brightly coloured scarves were laid out, there a collection of shoes and boots of all kinds, often in very poor condition. Elsewhere hangers bore crumpled suits in various sizes, old-fashioned rustic smocks and jackets, along with darned stockings, socks and shirts, hats and hairnets, all on sale and jumbled up together.'[11] However, the lowered standard of living and reduced economic conditions that are evident as the empirical foundations of the narrative in such passages are not the central constituents of Kasack's novel, which by and large mythologizes the reality as it was or could be experienced. But the critical potential of the type of fiction developed by Kasack, which is concerned with the complex insight that even those who survive collective catastrophes have already experienced their death, is not realized on the level of myth in his narrative discourse; instead, and in defiance of the sobriety of his prose style, Kasack aims to present a skilful irrationalization of the life that has been destroyed. The air raids which caused the destruction of the city appear, in a pseudo-epic style reminiscent of Döblin, as transreal entities. 'As if at the prompting of Indra, whose cruelty in destruction surpasses the demonic powers, they rose, the teeming messengers of death, to destroy the halls and houses of the great cities in murderous wars, a hundred times stronger than ever before, striking like the apocalypse.'[12] Green-masked figures, members of a secret sect who give off a stale odour of gas and may be meant to symbolize murdered concentration camp victims, are introduced (with allegorical exaggeration) in dispute with the bogeymen of power who, blown up to over life-size, proclaim a blasphemous dominion, until they collapse in on themselves, empty husks in uniform, leaving behind a diabolical stench. In the closing passages of the novel an attempt to make sense of the senseless is added to this *mise en scène*, which is almost worthy of

Syberberg and owes its existence to the most dubious aspects of Expressionist fantasy. A venerable Master Mage sets out the complex preliminary doctrines of a combination of Western philosophy and Eastern wisdom. 'The Master Mage indicated that for some time the thirty-three initiates had been concentrating their forces on opening up and extending the region of Asia, so long cut off, for reincarnations, and they now seemed to be intensifying their efforts by including the West too as an area for the resurrection of mind and body. This exchange of Asiatic and European ideas, hitherto only a gradual and sporadic process, was clearly perceptible in a series of phenomena.'[13]

In the course of further pronouncements by the Mage, Kasack's alter ego is brought to realize that millions must die in this wholesale operation 'to make room for those surging forward to be reborn. A vast number of people were called away prematurely, so that they could rise again when the time came as a growing crop, apocryphally reborn in a living space previously inaccessible to them.'[14] The choice of words and terminology in such passages, speaking of the opening up 'of the region of Asia, so long cut off', of the benefit of 'European ideas', and 'living space [*Lebensraum*] previously inaccessible' show with alarming clarity the degree to which philosophical speculation bound to the style of the time subverts its good intentions even in the attempt at synthesis. The thesis frequently held by the 'internal emigrants' that genuine literature had employed a secret language[15] under the totalitarian regime is thus proved true, in this as in other cases, only in so far as its own code accidentally happened to coincide with Fascist style and diction. The vision of a new educational field proposed by Kasack, as it also was by Hermann Hesse and Ernst Jünger, makes little difference to that fact, for it too is only a distortion of the bourgeois ideal of an association of the elect operating outside and above the state, an ideal which found its ultimate corruption and perfection in the officially ordained Fascist elites. When it seems to the archivist at the end of his story, then, 'as if a sign formed in the place that the departed spirit had touched with its finger, a small stain, a final rune of fate',[16] we are looking at an example that can hardly be surpassed of the tendency developing in Kasack's work, against his narrative intention, to bury the ruins of the time under the lumber of an equally ruined culture once again.

Even Hans Erich Nossack's description of the destruction of Hamburg, 'Der Untergang', which, as we shall see, gives a much more exact account of the real features of a collective catastrophe, lapses here and there into the mythologizing approach to extreme social circumstances which had become almost habitual since the time of the First World War, when realism gave up the ghost. Here too the writer resorts to the arsenal of the apocalypse, speaking of peaceful trees transformed in the beam of searchlights into black wolves 'leaping greedily at the bleeding crescent moon', and of infinity blowing at its will through the shattered windows, sanctifying the human countenance 'as the place of transition for the eternal'.[17] Nowhere in Nossack, however, does this fateful rhetoric, obstructing our view of the technical enterprise of destruction, degenerate to the point where he compromises himself ideologically as a writer. It is undeniably to Nossack's credit that in his thinking and in the writing of this piece of prose, which in many respects is exceptional, he largely resists the style of the time. The view of an immemorial city of the dead which he presents is thus much closer to reality and has a value qualitatively different from the account of the same theme in Kasack's novel.

I saw the faces of those standing beside me in the vehicle as we drove down the broad road over the Veddel to the Elbe bridge. We were like a tourist party; all we needed was a loudspeaker and the explanatory chatter of a guide. And we were all at a loss, and could not take in the strangeness. Where once your eyes met the walls of buildings, a silent plain now extended to infinity. Was it a cemetery? But what beings had buried their dead there and then put chimneys on the graves? Nothing grew there but the chimneys emerging from the ground like monuments, like dolmens or admonitory fingers.

Did the dead lying below them breathe the blue ether through those chimneys? And where, among this strange undergrowth, an empty façade hung in the air like a triumphal arch, was it the resting place of one of their princes or heroes? Or was it the remnant of an aqueduct of the ancient Roman kind? Or was all this just the stage set for a fantastic opera?[18]

The monumental theatrical scene of a ruined city presented to an observer passing by reflects something of Elias Canetti's later comment on Speer's architectural plans: for all their evocation of eternity and their enormous size, their design contained within itself the idea of a style of building that revealed all its grandiose aspirations only in a state of destruction. The curious sense of exaltation that sometimes seems to overcome Nossack at the sight of the devastation in his native city is very appropriate to that observation. Only from its ruins does the end of the Thousand-Year Reich that intended to usurp the future become conceivable. The emotional conflict arising from the fact that total destruction coincided with his personal liberation from an apparently hopeless situation was not, however, something that Nossack could reduce to a common denominator. In view of the utter catastrophe there seems to be something scandalous about the 'feeling of happiness' that he experiences on the drive 'towards the dead city' as something 'true and imperative', the need 'to cry out rejoicing: now, at last, real life begins',[19] and Nossack can justify it only by cultivating an awareness of shared guilt and responsibility. These circumstances also made it impossible for him to let his mind dwell on the agents of the destruction. Nossack speaks of a deeper insight that forbade him 'to think of an enemy who had done all this; he too was at most a tool of inscrutable powers that wanted to destroy us'.[20] Like Serenus Zeitblom* in his cell in Freising, Nossack feels that the strategy of the Allied air forces was the work of divine justice. Nor is this process of revenge solely a matter of retribution visited on the nation responsible for the Fascist regime; it is also concerned with the need for atonement felt by the individual, in this case the author, who has long yearned to see the city destroyed. 'In all earlier raids I wished clearly: let it be a very bad one! I felt it so very clearly that I might almost say I cried that wish aloud to heaven. It was not courage but curiosity to see if my wish would be granted that never let me go down to the cellar but held me spellbound on the apartment balcony.'[21] 'And if it is the case,' writes Nossack in another passage, 'that I called down the city's fate on it to force my own fate to its moment of decision, then I must also stand up and confess myself guilty of its fall.'[22] Such explorations of the conscience arise from the scruples of the survivors, their sense of shame at

*The narrator of Thomas Mann's Dr Faustus.

'not being among the victims',[23] and were later to feature among the central moral dimensions of West German literature. Reflections on the guilt of survival were probably presented most cogently by Elias Canetti, Peter Weiss and Wolfgang Hildesheimer,[24] which suggests that not much might have come of the process known in Germany as 'coming to terms with the past' but for the contribution made by writers of Jewish origin. There is further evidence in the fact that in the years following the fall of the Third Reich, the sense of guilt expressed by Nossack was initially transformed into an existential philosophy which still nurtured a belief in fate and endeavoured to face 'the void . . . with composure', a philosophy with a concept embracing personal failure, in which Nossack too sees 'the appropriate way of death for us'.[25] The crux of this resolution of the opposition between destruction and liberation lies in the fact that it upholds the promises of Death, which itself appears at the end of Nossack's text as an allegorical figure coming 'through the arch of the old gateway every afternoon',[26] enticing children out to play. The image of death as a companion of the writer's imagination is a metaphor for the mourning in which the population as a whole could not afford to indulge, as Alexander and Margarete Mitscherlich explained in their famous essay on the psychological disposition of the German nation after the catastrophe – for 'the mother of the family still has a great deal of work, she does the laundry, she cooks, and she must go down to the cellar from time to time to fetch coal'.[27] The ironic detachment here, complementing the melancholy of Nossack's narrative, demolishes the claim to the superior significance of death that pervades Kasack's novel, and does not deny those who managed to survive the right to a secular continuation of their existence.

Although in some of its amplifications Nossack's text goes beyond the plain facts of what happened, veering into personal confession and mythically allegorical structures, it may be understood in its entirety as a deliberate attempt to give as neutral as possible an account of an experience exceeding anything in the artistic imagination. In an essay of 1961 where Nossack speaks of the influences on his literary work, he writes that after reading Stendhal he was anxious to express himself 'as plainly as possible, without well-crafted adjectives, high-flown images or bluff, more like someone writing a letter in almost everyday jargon'.[28] This stylistic principle proves its worth in his depiction of the ruined city, in that it does not allow traditional literary methods which tend to homogenize collective and personal catastrophes; Mann's novel *Dr Faustus* is the contemporary paradigm. In direct contrast to the traditional approach to writing fiction, Nossack experiments with the prosaic genre of the report, the documentary account, the investigation, to make room for the historical contingency that breaks the mould of the culture of the novel. Where Kasack's book about the city beyond the river, which in its opening passages also tries to maintain the neutrality of an impersonal report, very soon lapses into features like those of fiction, Nossack manages to preserve, over long tracts of his work, the documentary tone that set an example for the later development of West German literature. If familiarity with social and cultural circumstances is the crucial prerequisite for both writing and reading novels, then the attitude of an agency that simply presents a report conveys a sense of reality that appears foreign. That is evident in Nossack's prose work 'Bericht eines fremden Wesens über die Menschen' ['Account of Mankind by a Strange Creature'], which is also associated with the themes described above and ascribes to the narrator the 'strangeness' in the title, but asks the reader whether the reason for it is not a mutation in mankind that makes the author an anachronistic figure. The wide distance between the subject and object of the narrative process implies something like the perspective of natural history, in which destruction and the tentative forms of new life that it generates act like biological experiments in which the species is concerned 'to break its mould and abjure the name of man'.[29] As the first sentence of his account tells us, Nossack witnesses the fall of Hamburg as

a spectator. Shortly before the air raid on the city of
21 July 1943 he had gone to spend a few days in a village
on the Lüneburg Heath, fifteen kilometres south of its
outskirts. The timelessness of the landscape reminds him
'that we come from a fairy tale and shall return to a fairy
tale again',[30] which in the circumstances suggests not
so much the idylls of Hermann Löns (the poet of that
area) as the precarious achievements of the technological
civilization that was shortly to return large parts of the
population to the hunter-gatherer stage of development.
From the Heath, the approaching destruction of the city
appears like a natural spectacle. Sirens howl 'like cats
somewhere in distant villages', the sound of the bomber
squadrons coming in hovers in the air 'between the clear
constellations and the dark earth', the shapes like 'fir
trees' dropping from the sky resemble 'red-hot drops of
metal flowing' down on the city, until they later disappear in a cloud of smoke, 'lit red from below by
the fire'.[31] The scene thus suggested, still containing
aestheticized elements, already shows that a 'description' of the catastrophe from its periphery rather than
its centre is possible. If Nossack's text conveys only a
reflection of the inferno, his own real evidence begins
when the raid is over and the extent of the destruction
is gradually revealed to him. Even before his return to
Hamburg he is amazed by the 'constant coming and
going' that begins with the firemen hurrying to the city's

aid from nearby towns, and continues 'on all the streets of the region around . . . by day and by night' during the throng's

flight from Hamburg, no one knew where. It was a river for which there was no bed; almost silently but inexorably deluging everything, carrying disquiet along little rivulets and into the most remote villages. Sometimes fugitives thought they could cling to a branch and so get a footing on the bank, but only for a few days or hours, and then they threw themselves back into the torrent to let it carry them on. None of them knew that they carried restlessness with them like a sickness, and everything it touched lost its firm foundation.[32]

Later Nossack comments on his impression that the journeying of the countless throngs of people on the move daily was by no means necessary 'to salvage something or keep an eye open for relatives . . . Yet I would not like to call it mere curiosity. People simply had no central point . . . and everyone was afraid of missing something.'[33] The aimlessly panic-stricken conduct of the population reported here by Nossack corresponds to no social norms, and can be understood only as a biological reflex set off by the destruction. Victor Gollancz, who in the autumn of 1945 visited several cities in the British-occupied zone, including Hamburg, in order to make first-hand reports which would convince the British public of the necessity of rendering humanitarian aid, notes the same phenomenon. He describes a visit to the Jahn Gymnastics Hall, 'where mothers and children were spending the night. They were units in that homeless crowd that goes milling about Germany "to find relatives", they said, but really, or mainly, I was told, because a restlessness has come over them that just won't let them settle down.'[34] The extreme restlessness and mobility to which Gollancz testifies were the reactions of a species seeing itself cut off from its ways of escape, which biologically speaking always lay ahead of it, and as preconscious experience those reactions affected the new social dynamic developing out of the destruction. Böll, who understood the constant movement associated with the war as a very specific aspect of human misfortune, with peacefully settled populations returning to the nomadic way of life, ascribes the post-war West German liking for speed, and the passion for travel which drives people out of that country every year in great droves, to the experiences of a historical period when whole social groups were removed from the last secure factor in their lives, the places where they lived.[35] Literature tells us very little more about the archaic behaviour that broke through in this way. Nossack does indicate that 'the usual disguises' of civilization fell away as if of their own accord, and 'greed and fear showed themselves naked and unashamed'.[36] The reversion of human life to the primitive, starting with the fact that, as Böll remembered later, 'this state began with a nation rummaging in the refuse',[37] is a sign that collective catastrophe marks the point where history threatens to revert to natural history. In the midst of the ruined civilization, what life is left assembles to begin at the beginning again in a different time. Nossack notes how unsurprising it seems 'that people had lit small fires in the open, as if they were in the jungle, and were cooking their food or boiling up their laundry on those fires'.[38] There is not much comfort, however, in the fact that in Nossack's account the city, now reduced to a desert of stone, soon begins to stir, that trodden paths appear across the rubble, linking up – as Kluge remarks – 'to a faint extent with earlier networks of paths',[39] for it is not yet certain whether the surviving remnants of the population will emerge from this regressive phase of evolution as the dominant species, or whether that species will be the rats or the flies swarming everywhere in the city instead. The revulsion at this new life, at the 'horror teeming under the stone of culture'[40] to which Nossack gives expression in one of the most terrible passages of his text, is a pendant to the fear that the inorganic destruction of life by the firestorm which (according to Walter Benjamin's distinction between bloody and non-bloody violence) might yet be reconcilable with the idea of divine justice, will be followed by organic decomposition caused by flies and rats, to which in Kasack's book too the river drawing the line between life and death 'forms no barrier'.[41] Writing from such an extreme situation required a redefinition of the author's moral position, which for Nossack can be justified only by the necessity of rendering accounts, or as Kasack puts it the need 'to note certain procedures and phenomena before they fall into oblivion'.[42] In such conditions writing becomes an imperative that dispenses with artifice in the interests of truth, and turns to a 'dispassionate kind of speech', reporting impersonally as if describing 'a terrible event from some prehistoric time'.[43] In an essay he wrote on the diary of Dr Hachiya from Hiroshima, Elias Canetti asks what it means to survive such a vast catastrophe, and says that the answer can be gauged only from a text which, like Hachiya's observations, is notable for precision and responsibility. 'If there were any point,' writes Canetti, 'in wondering what form of literature is essential to a thinking, seeing human being today, then it is this.'[44] The ideal of truth contained in the form of an entirely unpretentious report proves to be the irreducible foundation of all literary effort. It crystallizes resistance to the human faculty of suppressing any memories that might in some way be an obstacle to the continuance of life. The outcast, says Nossack, 'dared not look back, since there was nothing behind him but fire'.[45] For that very reason, however, memory and the passing on of the objective information it retains must be delegated to those who are ready to live with the risk of remembering. It is a risk because, as the following parable by Nossack shows, those in whom memory lives on bring down upon themselves the wrath of others who can continue to live only by forgetting. He writes of survivors sitting round the fire one night:

Then one man spoke in his dream. No one understood what he was saying. But they were all uneasy, they rose, they left the fire, they listened fearfully to the cold dark around them. They kicked the dreaming man, and he woke. 'I have been dreaming. I must tell you what I dreamed. I was back with what lies behind us.' And he sang a song. The fire burned low. The women began to weep. 'I confess, we were human beings!' Then the men said to each other, 'If it was as he dreamed we would freeze to death. Let us kill him!' And they killed him. Then the fire burned hot again, and everyone was content.[46]

The reason for the murder of memory lies in the fear that Orpheus's love for Eurydice might, as Nossack puts it in another passage,[47] turn to a passion for the goddess of death; it knows nothing of the positive potential of melancholy. But if it is true that 'the step from mourning to being comforted is not the greatest step but the smallest',[48] then the proof is in that passage of Nossack's account where he remembers the truly infernal death of a group of people who burned in a bomb-proof shelter because the doors had jammed and coal stored in the rooms next to it caught fire. 'They had all fled from the hot walls to the middle of the cellar. They were found there crowded together, bloated with the heat.'[49] The laconic comment reminds us of the Homeric lines about the fate of the hanged maids: 'So the women's heads were trapped in a line, / nooses yanking their necks up, one by one / so all might die a pitiful, ghastly death . . . / they kicked up heels for a little – not for long.'[50] The comfort of language evoking pity takes the reader, in Nossack's text, in very concrete terms straight from the horror of that coal cellar into the following passage about the convent garden. 'We had heard the Brandenburg concertos there in April. And a blind woman singer performed; she sang: *Die schwere Leidenszeit beginnt nun abermals* – ["The time of suffering now begins once more"]. Simple and self-assured, she leaned against the harpsichord, and her unseeing eyes looked past those trivialities for which we already feared, past them and perhaps to the place where we now stood, with nothing but a sea of stones around us.'[51] Here again, of course, we have a construction – a metaphysical construction – placed on the meaning. But the way in which Nossack puts his hopes in the will to tell the truth, and helps to overcome the tension between two poles by his unemotive style, may justify such a conjecture.

*

Comparison of Kasack's novel with Nossack's factual account also shows that an attempt to write a literary account of collective catastrophes inevitably, if it is to claim validity, breaks out of the novel form that owes its allegiance to bourgeois concepts. At the time when these works were produced the implications for the technique of writing could not yet be foreseen, but they became increasingly clear as West German literature absorbed the debacle of recent history. Consequently, Alexander Kluge's highly complex and at first sight heterogeneous book *Neue Geschichten. Hefte 1–18* ['New Stories. Nos. 1–18'], published in 1977, resists the temptation to integrate that is perpetuated in traditional literary forms by presenting the preliminary collection and organization of textual and pictorial material, both historical and fictional, straight from the author's notebooks, less to make any claim for the work than as an example of his literary method. If this procedure undermines the traditional idea of a creative writer bringing order to the discrepancies in the wide field of reality by arranging them in his own version, that does not invalidate his subjective involvement and commitment, the point of departure of all imaginative effort. Indeed, the second of the 'new stories', describing the air raid of 8 April 1945 on Halberstadt, is a model in this respect, showing how personal involvement in collective experience, a crucial feature of Nossack's writing too, can be made at least a heuristically meaningful concept through analytic historical investigations, relating it to immediately preceding events and later developments, to the present and to possible future perspectives. Kluge, who grew up in Halberstadt, was thirteen years old at the time of the air raid. 'When a high-explosive bomb drops you notice it,' he says in his introduction to the stories, adding, 'On 8 April 1945 something of that kind fell ten metres away from me.'[52] Nowhere else in the text does the author refer directly to himself. The tone of his account of the destruction of his native town is one of research into the past; the traumatically shocking experiences to which those affected reacted with complex processes of amnesiac suppression are brought into a present reality shaped by that buried history. In precisely the opposite way from Nossack, Kluge's retrospective presentation of what happened follows not what the author saw with his own eyes, or what he may still remember of it, but events peripheral to his own existence past and present. For the aim of the text as a whole, as we shall see, depends on the fact that experience in any real sense was actually impossible in view of the overwhelming speed and totality of the destruction; it could be acquired only indirectly, by learning about it later.

*

Kluge's literary record of the air raid on Halberstadt is also a model of its kind from another objective viewpoint, where it studies the question of the 'meaning' behind the methodical destruction of whole cities, which authors like Kasack and Nossack either omit for lack of information and out of a sense of personal guilt, or endow with mystical significance as divine justice and long overdue punishment. If the strategy of the area bombing of as many German cities as possible could not be justified by military objectives, which can hardly be denied today, then as Kluge's book shows the special case of the horrible devastation of a medium-sized town, of no importance either strategically or to the war economy, must raise very serious questions about the factors determining the dynamic of technological warfare. Kluge's account contains an interview with a high-ranking Allied staff officer by a correspondent for the *Neue Zürcher Zeitung*. Both the officer and the journalist flew with the raid as observers. The section of the interview quoted by Kluge deals primarily with the question of 'moral bombing', which Brigadier General Williams explains by reference to the official doctrine on which the air raids were based. When asked, 'Do you bomb for moral reasons or are you bombing the enemy's morale?' he replies, 'We are bombing the enemy's morale. The population's will to resist must be broken by the destruction of their city.' When pressed further, however, he admits that morale does not seem to be affected by the bombs.

Obviously morale is not located in the head or here [he points to his solar plexus] but somewhere among the individuals or populations of the cities concerned. We have investigated that, and it's known to the staff . . . Obviously it's not in the head or the heart, and that makes sense anyway, since people who have been killed by the bombs aren't thinking or feeling anything. And people who escape a raid like that in spite of our best efforts clearly don't take their impressions of the disaster with them. They take all the luggage they can, but they seem to leave behind their instant impressions of the raid itself.[53]

While Nossack offers us no conclusions about the motives and reasons for the act of destruction, Kluge, both here and in his book on Stalingrad, tries to account for the organizational structure of such a disaster, showing how even when the facts have become clearer the catastrophe continues on its old course because of administrative apathy, and there is no chance of raising the difficult question of ethical responsibility.

Kluge's account begins by showing the total inadequacy of all those modes of behaviour socially pre-programmed into us in the face of a catastrophe which is irrevocably unfolding. Frau Schrader, an employee of long standing at the Capitol cinema in Halberstadt, finds the usual course of the Sunday programme – it has been maintained for years, and the movie showing today, 8 April, is an Ucicky film starring Wessely, Petersen and Hörbiger* – disrupted by the prior claims of a programme of destruction. Her panic-stricken attempts to create some kind of order and perhaps clear up the rubble in time for the two o'clock matinée tellingly illustrates the extreme discrepancy between the active and passive fields of action involved in the catastrophe, leading the writer and his readers to the quasi-humorous observation that 'the devastation of the right-hand side of the auditorium . . . [had] no meaningful or dramaturgical connection with the film being screened'.[54] There is similar irrationality in the description of a troop of soldiers sent as an emergency force to dig up and sort out '100 corpses, some of them badly mutilated, partly from the ground, partly from visible depressions in it that had once been part of a shelter',[55] with no idea of the purpose of 'this operation' in the present circumstances. The unknown photographer intercepted by a military patrol who claims that he wants 'to record the burning city, his own home town, in its hour of misfortune',[56] resembles Frau Schrader in following his professional instincts. The only reason why his declared intention of

*A film by the director Gustav Ucicky, starring the actors Paula Wessely, Peter Petersen and Attila Hörbiger. The film was called *Heimkehr* ['Homecoming'].

recording the very end is not absurd is that the pictures he took, which Kluge added to his text and numbered 1 to 6, have survived, as he could hardly have expected at the time. The women on watch in the tower, Frau Arnold and Frau Zacke, equipped with folding chairs, torches, thermos flasks, packets of sandwiches, binoculars and radio sets, are still dutifully reporting as the tower itself seems to move beneath them and its wooden cladding begins to burn. Frau Arnold dies under a mountain of rubble with a bell on top of it, while Frau Zacke lies for hours with a broken thigh until she is rescued by people fleeing from the buildings on the Martiniplan. Twelve minutes after the air raid warning, a wedding party in the Zum Ross inn is buried, together with all its social differences and animosities – the bridegroom was 'from a prosperous family in Cologne', his bride, from Halberstadt, 'from the lower town'.[57] These and many of the other stories making up the text show how, even in the middle of the catastrophe, individuals and groups were still unable to assess the real degree of danger and deviate from their usual socially dictated roles. Since, as Kluge points out, normal time and 'the sensory experience of time' were at odds with each other, those affected 'could not have devised practicable emergency measures . . . except with tomorrow's brains'.[58] This divergence, for which 'tomorrow's brains' can never compensate, proves Brecht's dictum that human beings learn as much from catastrophes as laboratory rabbits learn about biology,[59] which in turn shows that the autonomy of mankind in the face of the real or potential destruction that it has caused is no greater in the history of the species than the autonomy of the animal in the scientist's cage, a circumstance that enables us to see why the speaking and thinking machines described by Stanislaw Lem wonder if human beings can actually think or are merely simulating that activity, and drawing their own self-image from it.[60]

Although it seems impossible, as a result of the socially and naturally determined human capacity to learn from experience, for the species to escape catastrophes generated by itself except purely by chance, studying the conditions in which destruction took place after the event is not pointless. Instead, the retrospective learning process – and this is the *raison d'être* of Kluge's account, compiled thirty years after the incidents he describes – is the only way of deflecting human wishful thinking towards anticipation of a future not already governed by the fears arising from suppressed experience. The primary school teacher Gerda Baethe, a character in Kluge's text, has similar ideas. It is true, the author comments, that to implement a 'strategy from below' such as Gerda has in mind would have required '70,000 determined school teachers, all like her, each of them teaching hard for twenty years from 1918 onwards, in every country that had fought in the war'.[61] Despite the ironic style, the prospect suggested here of an alternative historical outcome, possible in certain circumstances, is a serious call to work for the future in defiance of all calculations of probability. Central to Kluge's detailed description of the social organization of disaster, which is pre-programmed by the ever-recurrent and ever-intensifying mistakes of history, is the idea that a proper understanding of the catastrophes we are always setting off is the first prerequisite for the social organization of happiness. However, it is difficult to dismiss the idea that the systematic destruction Kluge sees arising from the development of the means and modes of industrial production hardly seems to justify the abstract principle of hope. The construction of the air war strategy in all its monstrous complexity, the transformation of bomber crews into professionals, 'trained administrators of war in the air', the necessity of countering, as far as possible, any personal perceptions they might have such as 'the neat and tidy fields below them, or any confusion of the sight of urban streets and squares with impressions of home', and of overcoming the psychological problem of keeping the crews interested in their tasks despite the abstract nature of their function, the problems of conducting an orderly cycle of operations involving '200 medium-sized industrial plants'[62] flying towards a city, the technology ensuring that the bombs would cause large-scale fires and firestorms – all these factors, which Kluge studies from the organizers' viewpoint, show that so much intelligence, capital and labour went into the planning of such destruction that, under the pressure of all the accumulated potential, it *had* to happen in the end. The central point of Kluge's comments is to be found in a 1952 interview between the Halberstadt journalist Kunzert, who had gone west with the British troops in 1945, and Brigadier Frederick L. Anderson of the US Eighth Army Air Force. In this interview Anderson tries, with some patience, to answer what from the professional military viewpoint is the naive question of whether hoisting a white flag made from six sheets from the towers of St Martin's church in good time might have prevented the bombing of the city. His comments, initially dealing with military logistics, culminate in a statement illustrating the notorious irrationality to which rational argument can lead. He points out that the bombs they had brought were, after all, 'expensive items'. 'In practice, they couldn't have been dropped over mountains or open country after so much labour had gone into making them at home.'[63] The result of the prior claims of productivity, from which, with the best will in the world, neither responsible individuals nor groups could dissociate themselves, is the ruined city laid out before us in one of the photographs included in

Kluge's text. The caption he gave it is from Marx: 'We see how the history of *industry* and the now *objective* existence of industry have become the *open* book of the *human consciousness*, human *psychology* perceived in sensory terms . . .' (Kluge's italics).

The reconstruction that Kluge was thus able to make of the disaster, in far more detail than the summary of it given here, can be likened to the revelation of the rational structure of something experienced by millions of human beings as an irrational blow of fate. It almost seems as if Kluge were responding to the question put by the allegorical figure of Death in Nossack's *Interview mit dem Tode* ['Interview with Death'] to his interlocutor: 'If you like you can see how I go about my business. There's no secret to it. The fact that there is no secret is the point. Do you understand me?'[64] Death, introduced to us in this text as a suave entrepreneur, explains to his listener, with the same ironic patience as is evident in Brigadier Anderson's attitude, that fundamentally everything is just a question of organization, and organization manifested not merely in the collective catastrophe but in all areas of daily life, so that to find out its secret all you need to do is visit a tax office or some similar civil service department. In Kluge's work, this very link between the vast extent of the destruction 'produced' by human beings and the realities we experience daily is the point upon which the author's didactic intention turns. Kluge reminds us all the time, and in every nuance of his complex linguistic montages, that merely maintaining a critical dialectic between past and present can lead to a learning process which is not fated in advance to come to a 'mortal conclusion'. The texts with which Kluge seeks to promote this aim correspond, as Andrew Bowie has pointed out,[65] neither to the pattern of retrospective historiography nor to the fictional story, nor do they try to offer a philosophy of history. Instead, they are a form of reflection on all these methods of ours for understanding the world. Kluge's art, to use the term in another way here, consists in using *details* to illustrate the main current of the dismal course so far taken by history. For instance, there is his mention of the fallen trees in the Halberstadt town park, 'where silk-moth caterpillars had lived when they were planted in the eighteenth century', and the following passage:

(Number 9 Domgang) In the windows stood a selection of tin soldiers, which had fallen over immediately after the raid, the rest of them being packed away in boxes stored in cupboards, 12,400 men in all, Ney's Third Corps as they desperately advanced through the Russian winter towards the eastern stragglers of the Grande Armée. They were put out on display once a year, during Advent. Only Herr Gramert himself could arrange the company of soldiers in their correct order. In his terrified flight, leaving his beloved soldiers, he has been struck on the head by a burning beam, and can form no further plans. The apartment at Number 9 Domgang, with all its marks of Gramert's personal style, lies quiet and intact for another two hours, except that it grows hotter and hotter during the afternoon. Around five o'clock it catches fire and so do the tin soldiers, who melt into lumps of metal in their boxes.[66]

A briefer didactic fable than this could hardly be written. Kluge's way of providing his documentary material with vectors through his presentation of it transfers what he quotes into the context of our own present. Kluge 'does not allow the data to stand merely as an account of a past catastrophe,' writes Andrew Bowie; 'the most unmediated document . . . loses its unmediated character via the processes of reflection the text sets up. History is no longer the past but also the present in which the reader must act.'[67] The information that Kluge's style thus imparts to readers about the concrete circumstances of their present existence, and possible prospects for the future, marks him out as an author who, on the perimeter of a civilization to all appearances intent on its own end, is working to revive the collective memory of his contemporaries who 'with the obviously inborn desire for narrative, [have] lost the psychological power to remember even within the destroyed city itself'.[68] It seems likely that only his preoccupation with this didactic business enables him to resist the temptation to offer an interpretation of recent historical events purely in terms of natural history, just as elements of the science fiction genre which knows all along what the end will be appear again and again in his work. Instead, he interprets history in a way rather like, for instance, Stanislaw Lem's: as the catastrophic consequence of an anthropogenesis based from the first on evolutionary mistakes, a consequence that has long been foreshadowed by the complex physiology of human beings, the development of their hypertrophic minds, and their technological methods of production.

Constructs of Mourning

Günter Grass and Wolfgang Hildesheimer

I. The Inability to Mourn. Deficiencies in Post-War Literature

And if the burthen of Isaac were sufficient for an holocaust, a man may carry his owne pyre.

Sir Thomas Browne, *Hydriotaphia, Urne-Buriall, or A Brief Discourse of the Sepulchrall Urnes lately found in Norfolk,* London, 1658

Alexander and Margarete Mitscherlich's theory of 'the inability to mourn', first formulated in 1967, has since proved[1] – although statistically this can hardly be verified – to be one of the clearest explanations given for the mental disposition of post-war society in West Germany. The absence 'of reactions of mourning after a national catastrophe of vast extent', the 'striking paralysis of feeling which was the response to the mountains of corpses in the concentration camps, the disappearance of the German armies into imprisonment, the news of the murder of millions of Jews, Poles and Russians, and political opponents from the ranks of the German people themselves', left negative impressions on the internal life of the new society, with consequences that can be properly understood only now, seen in the more distant retrospect of, say, the films of Fassbinder and Kluge.

The Mitscherlichs' theory of the distorted mental attitude of Federal German society as it took shape finds support not least – although they do not mention this – in the fact that attempts were actually made to organize collective mourning. The inept institutions of National Remembrance Day and German Unity Day, when during the Cold War years people were supposed to put candles in their windows for their brothers and sisters in the East, were ill-judged acknowledgements that there had been no natural reactions of mourning, so that the state had, as it were, to create them by decree. The imposition of mourning on a country that could no longer afford to indulge in a national day of celebration was the first sign that the Germans had managed to avoid a phase of collective melancholy (whose objective correlate would have wrecked the Morgenthau Plan),[2] instead bringing their psychological energies to bear 'on resisting the experience of a melancholy impoverishment of the self'.

The Mitscherlichs showed that 'the moral duty of

mourning for the victims of our ideological aims . . . for the time being could be only a superficial intellectual phenomenon', since in the circumstances the emotional collapse that psychologists might have expected had been displaced by mechanisms and strategies 'very close to the protective biological strategy for survival, if not actually analogous to it'.[3] While there was any perceptible questioning from outside of the nation's right to exist, and while the population's concrete needs stood in the way of preoccupation with their own guilt, then mourning and melancholy – both of which can be allowed expression only against a reasonably secure social background – were suppressed. That is why Alexander and Margarete Mitscherlich themselves do not set out to accuse the nation of psychologically inadequate reactions in the years directly after the end of the war because of the absence of mourning. What they do consider a problem is the fact that 'even later there was no proper mourning for our fellow human beings, killed in such great numbers by our own deeds'. That deficiency is perhaps most obvious in the literature written some ten or twelve years after currency reform, which shows hardly any insight into ideas of collective guilt and the need to describe the wrong that had been done. In many novels of the 1950s, for instance, egocentric sentimentality and criticisms of the new society which fall rather short of the mark are substitutes for the study of what happened to others among us. It is probably therefore fair to say that the authors of the 1950s, predestined to be the conscience of the new society, were as deaf to conscience as that new society itself.

NOSSACK: AN EXCEPTION

Among the few post-war writers who felt scruples about what had happened, and tried to articulate them in a form still relevant today, is Hans Erich Nossack. In his notes made at the time, he says a great deal about the responsibility of the survivors for their younger brothers, the shame of not being among the victims, sleepless nights, the necessity of thinking things out to the end, and failure as the proper way for us to die.[4] Nossack tried to understand the various categories of mourning through the example of Greek tragedy, and he realized that in a society which is too deeply afraid of feeling guilt to look back, if it is to conserve what vital energies it has left, in such a society anyone who mentions 'what lies behind us' is likely to be condemned by the general public.[5] Earlier than most others, Nossack understood where the difficulty of post-war writing chiefly lay: in the fact that memory was shameful and anyone who did remember would, like Hamlet, be admonished by the new men in power.

> *Do not for ever with thy vailed lids*
> *Seek for thy noble father in the dust:*
> *Thou know'st 'tis common; all that lives must die,*
> *Passing through nature to eternity.*[6]

These rather diplomatic words from the queen, who feels both concern for her son and the fear of discovery, are followed by the new king's more explicit warning that to continue mourning is 'impious stubbornness', from which we may conclude that in a political community which bears a heavy burden of guilt, wishing to remember the victims that preceded its establishment is the same thing as expressing doubts of the legitimacy of the new order, which must ignore the past and identify with the victors.

WISHFUL THINKING

While Nossack was trying to maintain a position of profound scepticism like Hamlet's against the consensus of society at large, most of the outstanding writers of the new Federal Republic (for instance Richter, Andersch and Böll) were already busy propagating the myth of the good German who had no choice but to let everything wash over him and bear it. At the heart of the apologia thus circulated was the fiction of a difference between passive resistance and passive collaboration, one that was in some way important.

As a result, in most literary works of the 1950s,

which are quite often decked out with a love story in which a good German man meets a Polish or Jewish girl, the incriminating past is 'reappraised' sentimentally rather than emotionally, and simultaneously the author extensively and successfully avoids – as the Mitscherlichs note in the case history appended to their essay – saying any more about the victims of the Fascist system.[7] If in individual psychological cases this course of action serves 'to keep signs of affection that are in short supply anyway within the pattern of family roles',[8] then in literature it maintains traditional narrative forms which could not convey an authentic attempt to mourn by identifying with the real victims.

Mitscherlich rightly complains that we, the readers, who would have liked to know more about the conflicts of the survivors and be given a more honest account of them, must put up with poorly drawn figments of wishful thinking personifying innocence, characters who can bear life among their opportunistic countrymen only as isolated individuals retreating, with resignation, into a private existence without any obligations, even though we know that such noble heroes do not usually exist.[9] 'The gulf between literature and politics in our country is as wide as ever,' so Mitscherlich sums it up in the middle of the 1960s, 'and so far none of our writers seems to have succeeded in influencing the political awareness and social culture of the Federal Republic one iota with his works.'[10]

Mitscherlich's diagnosis of the inherent inadequacies of German post-war literature, which at this time was undoubtedly correct, does not register the fact that since the beginning of the 1960s, and at least since the appearance of Hochhuth's in many respects devastating play *Der Stellvertreter* ['The Representative'], several authors had begun auditing the balance sheet of German guilt.

We may account for the delay before they did so not least by remembering that the real dimensions of the genocide perpetrated by their nation were only just beginning to dawn upon men of letters unused to factual research, and the legal reconstruction of the circumstances of that mass crime had itself been delayed. The minds of authors who would be important in the further development of West German literature began to be politicized to the same extent as the legal procedures culminating in the Auschwitz trial in Frankfurt shed light on the functionalism of a 'pedantically controlled apparatus of human destruction'.[11] *Die Ermittlung* ['The Investigation'], by Peter Weiss, whose road to Damascus the Frankfurt trial was, is one indication of that fact, and so are the *Frankfurter Vorlesungen* ['Frankfurt Lectures'] given in the mid 1960s by Heinrich Böll. They say more about Germany and the Germans, and say it more cogently, than anything in Böll's previous literary works.

Here for the first time Böll speaks, with his by now characteristic honesty and immediacy, of the lengthy emergence of recognition and emancipation in a country where 'too many murderers [go about] freely and boldly', people 'of whom it can never be proved that they are guilty of murder'. And he continues: 'Guilt, remorse, penance, insight, have not become social and certainly not political categories.'[12] However, he does not say that literature itself fended off possible insights longer than was good for it, and that the political and social immobility and provincialism that Mitscherlich connects directly with the 'doggedly maintained resistance to memories'[13] had its counterpart in literary immobility and provincialism.

Just as the nation as a whole concentrated all its energy and its entrepreneurial spirit 'on restoring what had been destroyed, extending and modernizing our industrial potential all the way to kitchen fittings', so the literature of the fifties, in a kind of parallel process, was notable less for a desire to investigate the truth than for a certain resentment of the miracles achieved in the economy; a situation diagnosed by Mitscherlich as 'political apathy with, simultaneously, a high degree of emotional stimulation in the field of consumption'.[14]

Deliberately taking sides against political apathy instead of merely deploring the lack of foundation for this parallel to 'Father Malachy's Miracle'* was to a great

*The title of a novel of 1931 filmed by the Austrian director Bernhard Wicki in 1961; the plot concerns the miraculous removal of a dance hall called The Garden of Eden from the city where it is giving offence.

extent the task of West German *literati* in the sixties. It provided them with their true *éducation sentimentale* as independent writers. These years of apprenticeship then found political expression in the commitment of many authors to political parties in the 1969 election.

This political commitment openly faced the question of the authenticity of democracy in Germany, where, as Böll has often reminded us, too swift and enthusiastic a readiness for reform aroused doubts of its real political substance. The commitment of Heinrich Böll and Günter Grass in the 1969 election was determined not least by the suspicion that their West German fellow countrymen would have been satisfied with a Christian Democratic Unity Party continuing into the future, from which they concluded that it was crucially important to the further development of democracy in Germany for the Social Democrats to come to power.

II. *Günter Grass: From the Diary of a Snail*

The outstanding feature of the history of the 1969 campaign is the elation felt when the Social Democrats just snatched victory; once again, the true line of democracy in the Federal Republic was identified with the long march of the Social Democrats, and not least with the role played by the literary figures who forged ahead in the last phase of that arduous journey. Part of the sum total of this experience was the realization, now consolidated, that democracy is concerned with more than a healthy economy. Grass apostrophizes it in his *Diary* by taking the popular clichés of the time expressing the nation's new self-confidence and incorporating them in his text as quotations:

'. . . and now after twenty-five years. From rubble and ashes we. From scratch. And today we are once more. Without false modesty. As the whole world is forced to. No one expected it. We can hold up our . . .'
    Yes, indeed. Storey on storey, and cost a pretty. Money in the bank all the same. Everything runs, flows, conveys, and lubricates itself automatically. Not just the victor powers, God himself comes to us for credit. We are again, somebody again, we are . . .'[15]

The question raised through this synoptic ridicule is directed at the nation's mental identity and, as the collage effect of the *Diary* makes clear in its first pages, can be answered only by presenting the experience of success in the present together with the debit entries, still not correctly deciphered, of our past.
    So this literary and political guide to the election campaign in Germany also becomes an account of the exodus of the Danzig Jews and the description of a place that had long remained a blank area on the map of

any work devoted to Danzig. Without the passages describing the fate of the persecuted minority, the *Diary of a Snail* would surely have remained a work written on a single level. For only the dimension of concrete remembrance lends substance to the central story of the schoolmaster nicknamed 'Doubt', and on another level substance to the reflections on melancholy. The presentation of local history does not, as usual in texts about that act of genocide, deal with 'the Jews' in a sense that, however terrifying, is abstract; instead the author and with him the reader understands that Jews from Danzig, Augsburg and Bamberg once really were fellow citizens and fellow human beings, and did not exist merely as a nebulous collective.

THE FATE OF THE DANZIG JEWS

We owe the story of the Danzig Jews as Grass tells it not primarily to the work of the author himself, knowledgeable as he is about the history of Danzig, but to the Jewish historian Erwin Lichtenstein. It is quite surprising to reflect that Grass – if his own text is correctly understood here – may in a way have come by the story gratis. 'On my visit to Israel from November 5 to November 18, 1971,' writes Grass in a parenthesis in the *Diary*, 'Erwin Lichtenstein informed me that his documents on ''The Exodus of the Jews from the Free

City of Danzig'' were soon to be published in book form by Mohr in Tübingen.'[16] And in fact the impressively real details that lend authenticity to the account of the journey of the Danzig Jews travelling from their home into exile and from exile home again derive almost exclusively from Lichtenstein's research.

We may leave aside the question of when, in developing his concept, Grass incorporated the exodus of the Jewish community of Danzig into the plan for his book. It is certain, however, that this chapter in the 'dark, complicated story' of which the narrator of *Cat and Mouse* says that it is not to be written by him 'and in no case in connection with Mahlke'[17] could not ultimately be written by Grass himself, for German *literati* still know little of the real fate of the persecuted Jews. But as, to employ an image of Canetti's, like all writers they follow their noses over the chasms of time, they now, as Grass himself puts it, have come home with 'the sniffed insight that it smells everywhere, and not only in quaint one-family houses, that sometimes frankly and pungently, sometimes lavender-sweetened, here masked by refrigeration, there streaked with mold, and next door unspeakably, it stinks, because here, there and next door the cellars harbor corpses.'[18]

Discovering the truth is thus shown to be the business of the dog described by Benjamin as the emblematic beast of melancholy, which as Kafka too knew 'symbolizes the darker aspect of the melancholy' as well as its 'tenacity'.[19]

'A writer,' says Grass, reflecting with melancholy on his own profession, 'a writer, children, is a man who loves fug and tries to give it a name, who lives on fug by giving it a name; a mode of life that puts calluses on the nose.'[20] Despite this almost constitutional compulsion of the man of letters to carry out research, noted by Mitscherlich, 'the real people we were ready to sacrifice to our master race have not yet appeared before the perception of our senses.'[21] The fact that Grass succeeded in making up some of that deficit in his *Diary* is something he owes primarily to the efforts of a historian living in Tel Aviv, and that in its own turn shows that literature today, left solely to its own devices, is no longer able to discover the truth.

THE CHARACTER OF HERMANN OTT

For this very reason the story of Hermann Ott that forms the backbone of the *Diary*, and is used by the author to offer the reader's receptive imagination many consoling ideas, will not ultimately stand up to critical examination. Unlike the documentary passages about the exodus of the Jews and the electoral campaign, the writer's own family life, and the essay-like digressions, it is pure invention, although everything else relates to it. This fact, of course, is initially disguised by the repeated suggestion that we really have here an incident from the life of Marcel Reich-Ranicki which cannot at present be made public.

Hermann Ott, nicknamed Doubt, by trade a teacher and a sceptic, has been teaching at the Rosenbaum private school since state schools were closed to the Jewish children of Danzig, and still buys his lettuce from Jewish tradesmen even when the market women call him names for it. This Hermann Ott is a retrospective figure created by the author's wishful thinking; structurally no different, if of far less fateful import, than the angelic young Father Riccardo Fontano in Hochhuth's *The Representative*, who provides evidence that good still exists even in the face of mass annihilation.

In order to leave Hermann Ott's German identity in no doubt, Grass gives us his literary alter ego's Aryan family tree of all the way back to Groningen in the Netherlands during the sixteenth century. The implication here, as in everything we learn about Hermann Ott, is that there really were Germans of a better kind, a thesis that stakes its claim to a high degree of probability through the combination of fiction with the documentary material. Whether the good and innocent Germans leading their quiet, heroic lives in the country's post-war literature really existed in the way suggested to the reader probably matters less, objectively speaking, than the obvious fact that, as we can read in Böll, they confined their effective activities to saying a Good Friday prayer which 'even includes the unbelieving Jews'.[22]

German literature of the post-war period sought its moral salvation in these fictional figures, of whom Günter Grass's Doubt is certainly one of the most honourable, and, thus preoccupied, failed to understand the grave and lasting deformities in the emotional lives of those who let themselves be integrated into the system without questioning it.

The invented figure of the teacher Doubt, enabling Grass to develop his snail-theme of melancholy, thus functions as an alibi to counter the programmatic intention of mourning, and the real aspects of the story of the Danzig Jews once again fail to get their due, despite the aid of Erwin Lichtenstein. One of the passages in the *Diary* where an appearance of truth is created by the confrontation of historical reality and retrospective fiction is a passage about the transports taking those Jewish children who were able to leave Danzig to England. Faced with his own children's questions:

'Did they have to go to school, too?'
'Did they all learn English quick?'
'And what about their parents?'
'Where did they go?'[23]

Grass responds by telling them about an English journalist who came from Danzig and had accompanied him for part of the electoral campaign. To this journalist, who left Danzig at the age of nearly twelve on one of the children's transports, pictures of his native town were still clear: 'gables, churches, streets, porches, and chimes, gulls on blocks of ice and over brackish water – in chiaroscuro, like broken toys', but 'he couldn't remember a schoolteacher by the name of Ott (known as Doubt)'.[24] The situation thus sketched makes one wonder whether the dominance of fiction over what really happened does not tend to militate against the recording of the truth and the attempt to commemorate it.

THE SOCIAL DEMOCRATIC ELECTORAL CAMPAIGN

Another of the images of wishful thinking constructed by Grass in the *Diary of a Snail* is his idea of German Social Democracy, on behalf of which he undertakes all the stress and strain of a campaign trip covering 31,000 kilometres.

The first striking feature in this context is that while Grass likes to describe the prehistory and early history of Social Democracy, he says nothing about the political debacle brought about by the party in Germany in the years after the First World War. We see August Bebel in his green turner's apron, and 'Ede' Bernstein, and we are told that Willy Brandt now owns the watch that once belonged to the first party leader and that it is still in working order, details conveying a pleasing air of family solidarity with the representatives of an upright past, but we hear nothing of Ebert and Noske,* to name just two of the less glorious figures.

Nor is it explained to a younger generation of readers how a country which, in the late nineteenth century, produced the strongest and best-organized of all Socialist movements, came to fall into the arms of Fascism twenty to thirty years later. As Grass presents it, the historical background of Social Democracy is underexposed, merely adorned for effect with a few picturesque details and brave figures such as that of the upright Bebel travelling illegally through the country and setting the comrades an example under the anti-Socialist laws, thus of course helping the campaign of the new pioneers of Social Democracy to appear in a somewhat heroic light.

From time to time a sense of fraternity in a common cause spreads among the generation of 'quadragenarians' who hope for a new political dawn and who, Grass thinks, 'seem to be trying to compensate by overproduction for the reduced achievement of a few decimated war years'.[25] The reader almost feels that the author finds absolution for what still irks him about the German

---

*Friedrich Ebert (1871–1925) was the first President of the Weimar Republic, and had become chairman of the Social Democratic Party in 1913. Gustav Noske (1868–1946) was also a prominent politician during the Weimar Republic period.

past, although he knows himself innocent of it, in his practical commitment to a better German political system, and that only in active politics and the hectic haste of travelling – identified by Böll in his *Frankfurt Lectures* as a particularly German form of desperation – can he keep a little way ahead of those resolute, monosyllabic snails Guilt and Shame.[26]

DÜRER'S MELANCHOLY

If the political activity in which, as Grass constantly emphasizes, he sees something more real than the construction of utopian plans, thus succeeds in warding off a despair that is moving in itself, then Dürer's Melancholia has made her way into his travelling bag as fellow traveller and angel of his guilty conscience.

That monstrous lady in whom a dog lies buried, and whose draped garment covers the stench of the whole country, 'with clammy fingers . . . holds the compass and cannot close the circle',[27] probably because – like the author himself – she is concerned, over and above the present task, with the problem of squaring morality implied by the question of whether by writing, and thus representing everyone else who does not write, he cannot make a contribution to the therapy of the nation, rather as Doubt cures his cold Lisbeth by the application of an 'unidentified slug'. The black gall or bile that this curiosity of nature magically draws out of the depressive Lisbeth was, as Grass reminds us, still current in the sixteenth century as a synonym for the ink with which the writer draws his circles. However, a writer who uses black bile as a medium for creative work risks taking on the misunderstood depression of those for whom he writes.

The further course of Doubt's story illustrates this very forcefully. After he has proved 'that melancholia is curable' – by means of a suction slug – the author condemns him to twelve years in a mental hospital where he lives forgotten, 'muttering over the jumbled handwriting on his papers'[28] until, we do not know how, he himself is cured and finds a niche as a cultural affairs official in Kassel in West Germany.

If we ignore this too optimistic turn in the plot, the story tells us that in the social system of the division of labour it is the writer squaring morality who overcomes the collective conscience, and like Dürer in his self-portrait (cited in Grass's text) points his right finger to the site of illness in his pen-and-ink drawing, adding the words: 'Where the yellow spot is and where the finger is pointing, that is where it hurts.'[29]

In choosing Dürer's demonstration of suffering as the emblem of his own philosophy of mourning, Grass transcends the question of whether melancholy is a constitutional or a reactive condition, a question which ultimately cannot be clinically determined. It may be true that the chronicle of Grass's journey through Germany would have been a far less intelligent book without that contrapuntal excursus into mourning, but it is equally true that there is something laboriously constructed about the excursus, making it rather like the performance of a historical duty.

III. Wolfgang Hildesheimer: Tynset

In contrast, Wolfgang Hildesheimer's novel *Tynset*, which has had nothing like the attention and recognition that its inherent qualities should receive, seems to have been created from the heart of mourning itself.

THE ANONYMOUS VOICE
OF CONSCIENCE

The story of the first-person narrator of this lengthy monologue, who is tormented by insomnia and melancholy and is never clearly perceived as a character, only as a voice, begins at a time (somewhere in the post-war years) when he was still trying to live in Germany, 'where the superannuated and retired criminals, now too old for prosecution' appear to lead their lives unchallenged 'among their children, their in-laws and their grandchildren'.[30] Uneasy and disturbed by what he, like

Hamlet, recognizes as a state of unsanctified legitimacy, the nameless narrator, who likes to leaf through telephone directories at night, cannot resist the temptation to pursue the sense of complicity and fellow-travelling that lurks hidden everywhere in the country. First at random, then more systematically following the trails that emerge from his random samples, he conveys to a series of upright fellow citizens the information that all is discovered, causing those who receive so urgent a message to leave home in haste, perhaps with a violin case under the arm, and disappear over the horizon like Kleist's corrupt village judge Adam after the identity of the person who broke the jug has been discovered.

In pursuing these activities the narrator, almost by chance, becomes an anonymous arbiter of conscience to his guilt-ridden contemporaries, a role that he adopts almost playfully, and not without relishing the grotesque comedy he has set in motion, until his hyper-sensitive ear that picks up the slightest sound one day hears the tell-tale crackle on his own telephone, and he knows that his own experimental system of persecution has turned against him.

NIGHTS LIKE HAMLET'S

At this he acutely feels 'the fear of the silence of the nights in which those beings that know no fear are at work', and he decides to escape it by moving 'to another country'.[31] This other country, from which he now continues his narrative, can be identified as a remote region of the Alps but remains, for the reader, as anonymous and undiscovered as the figure of the narrator himself; in the further course of the story, indeed, it turns out to be that bourn from which, as Hamlet knows, no traveller returns, and is thus a metaphor of exile and death. The protagonist, now living there in deep distress, speaks to us from the fixed abode of melancholy which he roams by night, entangled in the inescapable associations of a terrifying past which lies in wait for him on the stairs in the shape of Hamlet's father. But having understood the dialectic of victim and persecutor by means of his own experiment, he rejects the ghost's request for revenge, the better to preserve his awareness of his own innocence. He now uses the telephone with which he woke the guilty from sleep in Germany merely 'to listen, sometimes to listen only to the humming silence, the one sound made by passing time'.[32]

Moving on under the eye of Hamlet's father, who is waiting to grasp his little finger and then his whole hand, the narrator remembers his own father, 'killed by good Christian family men from Vienna or the Westerwald', who does not stand on the stairs 'looking for means of revenge'.[33] However, his own renunciation of revenge in emulation of this absent example does not exorcize the poor souls who walk by night, and he listens as intently and with as much longing for the crowing of the cocks as the Danish watchmen at the beginning of Shakespeare's play, for as everyone knows ghosts do not vanish until cockcrow.

But the narrator of *Tynset* is denied the pious Christian hope articulated in *Hamlet*:

> It faded on the crowing of the cock.
> Some say that ever 'gainst that season comes
> Wherein our Saviour's birth is celebrated,
> The bird of dawning singeth all night long[34]

bringing the prospect of final liberation from the nightmare of the past by salvation. Indeed, the Christian idea of hope seems to be finally discredited by the alcoholic misery of the housekeeper Celestina, who seeks absolution from the narrator in one of the many nocturnal scenes; by the figure of the Chicago evangelist Wesley B. Prosniczer, who also visits him unasked and later finds a cold grave in a snowdrift; and by a 1961 press cutting describing a defence minister about to kiss the ring on the hand that is offered to him by a cardinal. The crowing of the cock, then, does not here promise the dawning of a new day in any higher sense, merely a brief respite from the coming of the next of the many nights still to be endured, nights which – as Kafka noted – are divided into phases of waking and sleeplessness.[35]

This realization of the impossibility of salvation matches the unrelated condition of melancholy which, in developing its own rituals, promises some relief but not release from suffering and the 'feral deseases'[36] so often mentioned in Robert Burton's *Anatomy of Melancholy*. Among these rituals, in the narrator's case, are the nocturnal reading of telephone directories and timetables, the unfolding of maps and the making of plans for imaginary journeys to the most distant of lands, countries that might well lie beyond the sea shown in the background of Dürer's *Melencolia*. Like Robert Burton, who was familiar with melancholy all his life, the narrator is a man 'who delights in cosmography . . . but has never travelled except by map and card'.[37] And the summer bed with room enough for seven sleepers where he meditates on stories such as that of the Black Death, with all its paths and coincidences, is of the same century as Burton's compendium, an era of anxiety when the fear was first uttered 'that the great mutations of the world are acted, or time may be too short for our designes'.[38] The narrator's digressive excursions from the starting point of this realization open up the view – again, a reminiscence from *Hamlet* – of a world lying far below melancholy, a 'dead globe crawling with parasites'[39] whose power of attraction is spent and forfeit. The icy sense of distance as the narrator turns away from all earthly life represents a vanishing point in the dialectic of melancholy.

However, the other dimension of the Saturnian circumstances responsible for melancholy does point, as Benjamin has said, and in the context of the heavy, dry nature of that planet, to the type of man predestined to hard and fruitless agricultural labour.[40] It is probably no coincidence that the narrator's only utilitarian occupation seems to be growing herbs. He sends these herbs, dried and in carefully adjusted mixtures, to various delicatessen stores in Milan and Amsterdam as well as to Germany, to Hamburg and Hannover. Perhaps they bear the words 'Rosemary, that's for remembrance' written in Ophelia's hand.[41]

THE IDEAL OF LIGHTLESSNESS

This last, tenuous connection with the outside world also expresses the wish for a progressive and gradual removal from the society of mankind. It is complemented by a tendency towards dematerialization that in the text has its symbolical counterpart in a painting – a work which ranks very high in the narrator's estimation – so dark and black 'that it gives not the slightest idea of what it may once have shown'.[42] 'The ideal of blackness' of which this picture, signed by one Jean Gaspard Muller, is an example, is, as Adorno remarked in his *Ästhetische Theorie*, 'one of the deepest impulses of abstraction'.[43] To follow that impulse, to reach a place 'where no star, no light is visible, where there is nothing, where nothing is forgotten because nothing is remembered, where it is night, where it is nothing, nothing, void',[44] is the deepest emotion to move the narrator when, in the darkness, he explores the spaces between the stars with his telescope.

But as the narrator well knows, the search for the ideal of absolute lightlessness remains a hopeless undertaking, for the more he reduces the angle of his lens to exclude the stars still perceptible in his field of vision, the further he sees into the depths of space from which heavenly bodies previously darkened by distance now shine out. Here, then, we are dealing with something far from nihilism in the usual sense of the word; it is more like an approximation to death, that black point which, in the narrator's imagination, is always becoming 'blacker and thicker, ever thicker and ever longer', and to which his melancholy clings like 'the fat weed / That roots itself in ease on Lethe wharf',[45] a provocative gesture of resignation.

Melancholy of all entities will make no pact with death, for it knows him as 'the most gloomy representative of a gloomy reality'[46] and therefore, like the traveller who, at the beginning of *The Castle*, voluntarily crosses the bridge into unsurveyed country, speculates on whether death might not be vulnerable to an invasion of his own territory.

The area that melancholy thus sets out to explore stretches out before us in *The Castle* as a snowy, frozen landscape, and its exact counterpart is Tynset, a place in the north of Norway which the narrator ventures to visit. Tynset is the penultimate stage on his journey. After it comes Röros, which '[lies] like a last camp on the way to the end of the world, before that way is lost in inhospitable regions, a territory so incalculable, so menacing, that its exploration has been postponed year after year, until the camp has become eternal autumn quarters inhabited by ageing explorers who have lost sight of their goal; have forgotten it, and now look vaguely for the geographical origins of a melancholy . . . that they have long been seeking, but on which they can never lay hands.'[47]

THE COLD MAMSELL

The inhospitable region which the melancholy disposition adopts as its home in this reflection is its idea not just of the anteroom of death, but also of the place where we are all continually entertained by a sinister lady who, as Hildesheimer confided to his friend Max in a recently published letter, regularly awaits us after midnight. She is 'the Cold Mamsell', a name accurately denoting her profession, similarly remembered by Grass in evoking Dürer's *Melencolia*. Among her avocations – as Hildesheimer describes them with some malice – are rolling up salami slices and wrapping cold asparagus in strips of ham, arranging olives on savoury breadsticks, slicing cheese thinly, cutting gherkins into fan shapes, carving tomatoes into eights and radishes into water-lily shapes, splitting onions into rings, laying cubed brawn on platters and sliced cold meats on a bed of lettuce. So that Max will know just who he is dealing with, Hildesheimer adds to this description: 'You see, she comes from Germany. In line with her name, she is rather cold, especially her shoulders.'[48]

If anyone needs further information to identify this lady, let us add that we are already familiar with one of her sisters-in-law from Kafka's novel quoted above; she keeps house in the castle and 'it is usually cold in castles and always winter / for the sun of righteousness is far from them . . . so courtiers shiver with cold, / fear and sadness'.[49] That sister-in-law of the Cold Mamsell who presides over this draughty place can boast several chests of grand dresses, and whenever she, this Madame la Mort, goes to fetch someone she has a new one made, which she then adds to those already in her wardrobe, and consequently she also gives the surveyor the opportunity of entering her service as a tailor; a compromising offer which in view of his own mission he must decline.

Des Häschens Kind, der kleine Has
[The Little Hare,
Child of the Hare]
On the poet Ernst Herbeck's totem animal

Most of the recent literature we persist in reading seems inane only a few years later. Or at least, and so far as I am concerned, very little of it has stood the test of time as well as the poems written by Ernst Herbeck from around 1960 onwards in his mental hospital in Gugging.

I first came upon Herbeck's eccentric figures of speech in 1966. I remember sitting in the Rylands Library in Manchester reading a work on the calamitous Carl Sternheim, and every now and then, as if to refresh my mind, picking up the little volume published by dtv on *Schizophrenie und Sprache* ['Schizophrenia and Language'] and finding myself amazed by the brilliance of the riddling verbal images conjured up, evidently at random, by this most unfortunate of poets. Today, such sequences of words as *'Firn der Schnee das Eis gefriert'* ('Firn the snow the ice freezes') or *'Blau. Die Rote Farbe. Die Gelbe Farbe. Die Dunkelgrüne. Der Himmel ELLENO'* ('Blue. The

Red Colour. The Yellow Colour. The Dark Green. The sky ELLENO') still seem to me to verge on the frontiers of a breathless other world.

Again and again passages of slight distortion and gentle resignation remind one of the way in which Matthias Claudius sometimes manages, with a single semitone or pause, to induce a momentary feeling of levitation in the reader. Ernst Herbeck writes: 'Bright we read in the misty sky / How stout the winter days. Are.' There is probably no greater sense of both distance and closeness anywhere in literature. Herbeck's poems show us the world in reverse perspective. Everything is contained in a tiny circular image.

It is astonishing that over and beyond his own poems Herbeck also gave us a theory of poetics in a few statements of principle. 'Poetry,' he writes, 'is an oral way of shaping history in slow motion . . . Poetry is also antipathetic to reality, and weighs more heavily. Poetry transfers authority to the pupil. The pupil learns poetry; and that is the history in the book. We learn poetry from the animal in the woods. Gazelles are famous historians.'

Ernst Herbeck, who spent most of his life in a psychiatric hospital, hardly knew the contemporary history of Austria and Germany at first hand, but he remembered Adolf Hitler as Reich Chancellor, the enthusiasm with which Vienna received him, and other festive occasions of the past. A Christmas poem not only mentions the inevitable snow and lighted candles, but contains references to banners, warfare and downfall.

Wartime Christmas as Goebbels envisaged it, and as recalled to memory by Kluge and Reitz, flares up again in Herbeck's poetry. A poem entitled 'Ins Stammbuch' ['Taken to Heart'] and beginning with the lines: *'Der Tag ist auf die gut Deutsche / Eiche Tot der vergangen Heid'* ('the day is risen the good German / oak Dead the departed heathen') gives us more to think about than does the professional disposal of our burden of guilt and the past. It seems to me actually uncanny that Herbeck wrote the following poem in that historic year 1989. I wish all my countrymen would take it to heart.

> *Das Schwert ist eine seriöse deutsche*
> *Waffe und wird von den Gothen und*
> *wird von den ausserstehenden Ger-*
> *manen verwendet; bis auf den*
> *heutigen Tag. Dies im gesamtdeu-*
> *tschen Raum (Germanien).*

> The sword is a serious German
> weapon used by the Goths and
> used by the Germanic peoples
> further afield; up to the
> present day. And this in the whole
> German area (Germania).

However, I do not mean to write about Ernst Herbeck's concept of national history here, but on his attempts to record the history of his own family and descent in complex mythological terms. In her book *Die Ver-rückung der Sprache* ['The Dis-placement of Language'], Gisela Steinlechner has shown that the work of Herbeck is full of anthropomorphic portraits of animals. One reason for this is that titles such as 'The Zebra' and 'The Giraffe' were often given to the poet by his psychiatrist as exercises, so that the patient could write about them. Since Herbeck in general kept closely to the subjects he was offered, he produced a whole bestiary – a child's primer confirming, if ironically, the general validity of the taxonomic order we have devised. 'The raven leads the devout', 'The owl loves children', 'The zebra runs through broad fields' and 'The kangaroo leans on its support' – none of this is very disturbing. Yet Herbeck also writes of unknown species not listed in zoological encyclopaedias, making us suspect that the animals are not so very different from each other, or we ultimately from them as we would like to think. We come upon a being that is half lamb, half cat in Herbeck, as we do in the synagogue mentioned by Franz Kafka.

Much more mysterious than these strange creatures, however, is the symbolic hare in Herbeck's work, a creature which the author related to the question of his own origin. He gives only the most cursory and singular facts about his early history. Everything to do with the family and relatives is a mystery to him. 'One question, please!' he writes. 'Are the son-in-law's children father-in-law to their siblings? I can't work it out! Please tell me, and thank you.' In fact to Herbeck, doomed to lifelong celibacy, the most inscrutable feature of these relationships was the idea of married life, on which he makes only a few vague and extremely innocent comments.

> *Die Ehe ist vorbildlich f. Mann und Frau*
> *in jeder Hinsicht. Sie wird meistens ein*
> *gegangen und gescholssen. Nach der Ver-*
> *lobung und. Je länger sie dauert desto*
> *kürzer und länger das Dasein. Eines Hasen*
> *oder so.*

> Marriage is the model for man and wife
> in every respect. You usually enter into
> it, you celebrate it. After the en-
> gagement and. The longer it lasts the
> shorter and longer the existence. Of a hare
> or suchlike.

What happens after that 'and' and the full stop is something the writer cannot or will not envisage. On the other hand, he knows that conjugal life may eventually produce a hare. It is not so easy to describe how the act of procreation works. Perhaps it is not so much a sexual act as a kind of spontaneous reproduction, even magic.

> *Der Zauberer zaubert Sachen:*
> *Kleine Hasen. Tücher. Eier.*
> *Er zaubert wiederholt.*
> *Er steckt das Tuch in den Zylinder*
> *und zieht es wieder heraus*
> *es ist ein zahmer Hase dabei.*

> The conjuror conjures things up:
> little hares. Scarves. Eggs.
> He keeps on doing magic.
> He puts the scarf in the top hat
> and brings it out again
> with a tame hare in it.

The hare so miraculously produced from the top hat is undoubtedly the totem animal in which the writer sees himself. The harelip with which he was born, and which was operated on several times, probably played a crucial part as a pre-morbid disability in the genesis and particular development of Herbeck's schizophrenia and the specific form it took. It is an identifying mark; in his mind, Herbeck takes this blemish much further back in time than his childhood. When he is asked to write a poem on 'The Embryo' he forgets that strange new word, and instead writes the following lines on an unborn fabulous animal more closely related to him, which he calls the 'empyrum'.

> *Heil unserer Mutter! Ein werdendes*
> *Kind in Leibe der Mutter. Als ich*
> *ein Empyrum war, hat sie mich*
> *operiert. Ich kann meine Nase*
> *nicht vergessen. Armes Empyrum.*

> Hail to the mother! A future
> child in the mother's womb. When I
> was an empyrum, she operated
> on me. I can't forget
> my nose. Poor empyrum.

Gisela Steinlechner, in her studies of the work of Ernst Herbeck, was the first to try to describe the pre-existential trauma that, to the damaged subject, later became his own myth. Among other sources, she drew on the three-page autobiographical account written by Herbeck in 1970, in which he describes how at the age of eleven he was in a Pathfinder group under a leader called Meier; their group was called the Pigeons, unlike the others, who were Eagles or Stags. The Pathfinders organization is one of the last in which human beings give themselves the names of totem animals, but this odd little fact is less important in itself than Herbeck's Pathfinder reminiscence of only a few lines which, in an entirely agrammatical context, uses the very odd word 'Thierenschaft' ('beastship'). The old German spelling *Thier* instead of modern *Tier* for 'animal' (the 'h' long ago became silent), suggests a time before human beings were even capable of speech.

Since in the history of our species ancient strategies of thinking and mental organization regularly occur in those described as mentally ill, it is not at all far-fetched to look back to the basic rules governing the totemic imagination in order to find out what Herbeck meant. Gisela Steinlechner has interpreted the harelip as the symbol upon which Herbeck himself fixed for his split personality. In this connection she looks at Claude Lévi-Strauss's proposition that in American Indian myths the harelip was the remaining trace of a twin who was never actually born. This duality in one person makes the hare, with its split face, one of the highest deities, mediating between heaven and earth. But part of the Messianic vocation is to be elect in the context of salvation, and at the same time ostracized and persecuted in the secular world. Not for nothing did Ernst Herbeck, who probably felt the grief of the despised more than any sense of mission as the Son of Man, place four exclamation marks after the title for a poem that he was given one day, 'The Hare'. The poem itself runs as follows:

Der Hase is ein kühnes Tier!
Er läuft bis ihm die Strappen
fassen. Die Ohren spitzgestellt; er
lauscht. Für ihn — ist keine Zeit
zum Rasten. Lauf läuft läuft.
Armer Hase!

The hare is a bold animal!
He runs until the snare
catches him. Ears pricked; he
listens. For him — there is no time
to rest. Run runs runs.
Poor hare!

The ambivalent nature of the hare in myth, closely combining power and impotence, boldness and fear, determines Herbeck's concept of the nature of his emblematic animal.

In his autobiographical essay he also tells us (as Gisela Steinlechner too has pointed out) that his mother 'had a hare' at what the author calls a time of revolt and the 'need for silver'. By saying that she had a hare (*einen Hasen bekam*) he means, of course, that she 'was brought or given' a hare, a useful addition to the meagre diet of the times. The brief phrase used by Herbeck, however, suggests that his mother 'had a hare' as a woman might have a baby.

This hare is then killed by his mother in his father's presence, and after that skinned. Herbeck does not mention the dish of roast hare itself, but adds at the close of his account of the incident only the confession, 'It tasted too good to me', which in a few words sums up the moral of the whole story. The true extent of his involvement in the dark machinations of social life is that he was involved in the joint family crime not just as victim but as perpetrator, having helped to consume his likeness and namesake. To those who can understand it, the legend of the poor hare used by Herbeck to explain his sad fate is an exemplary tale of suffering. 'The greater the suffering,' he once wrote, 'the greater the poet. The harder the work. The deeper the meaning.'

To the Brothel by way of Switzerland

On Kafka's travel diaries

A Dutch acquaintance recently told me how she travelled last winter from Prague to Nuremberg. During the journey she was reading Kafka's travel diaries, and sometimes spent a long time looking out at the snowflakes driven past the window of the old-fashioned dining car, which with its ruffled curtains and little table lamp spreading reddish light reminded her of the windows of a small Bohemian brothel. All that she remembered from her reading was the passage where Kafka describes one of his fellow travellers cleaning his teeth with the corner of a visiting card, and she remembered that not because the description was particularly remarkable, but because no sooner had she turned a few pages than a strikingly stout man sitting at the table next to hers also, and not a little to her alarm, began probing between his own teeth with a visiting card, apparently without any inhibitions at all. This story made me return, after I had not looked at them for a long time, to the notes that

Kafka made when he and Max Brod travelled from Prague to Paris by way of Switzerland and Northern Italy in August and September 1911. Much of that account is as real to me as if I myself had been there, and not just because 'Max' is so frequently mentioned, for instance when a lady's hat falls on him in the train compartment, or Franz leaves him alone 'sitting over a grenadine by himself in the darkness on the outskirts of a half-empty open-air café'; no, in a curious way the stages of that summer trip of the past taken by the two bachelors are more familiar to me than any other place at a later date. Even the car drive in the rain through Munich by night – 'The tyres make a rushing noise on the asphalt, like the whirr of a cinema projector' – bring back great tracts of the memory of my first real journey taken in 1948, when I and my father, who had just returned from a POW camp, went from W. to visit my grandparents in Plattling. My mother had made me a green jacket, and a little rucksack of check fabric. I think we travelled in a third-class compartment. On Munich station, where you could see huge mounds of rubble and ruins as you stood in the forecourt, I felt unwell and had to throw up in one of those 'cabins' of which Kafka writes that he and Max washed their hands and faces in them before boarding the night train which passed through the dark foothills of the Alps by way of Kaufering, Buchloe, Kaufbeuren, Kempten and Immenstadt to

Lindau, where there was a great deal of singing on the platform long after midnight, a situation I know very well, since there are always a number of drunks on Lindau station who have been out on excursions. Similarly, the 'impression of separate buildings standing very upright in St Gall, without being part of a street', but running along the slopes of the valley like one of Schiele's Krumau pictures, accurately corresponds to the scenery of a place where I lived for a year. In general, Kafka's comments on the Swiss landscape, the 'dark, hilly, wooded banks of Lake Zug' (and how often he writes of such things) remind me of my own childhood expeditions to Switzerland, for instance on a day trip we made by bus in 1952 from S. to Bregenz, St Gall and Zürich, along the Walensee, through the valley of the Rhine and home again. At the time there were comparatively few cars around in Switzerland, and because many of those were American limousines – Chevrolets, Pontiacs and Oldsmobiles – I really thought we were in some entirely foreign, quasi-utopian country, rather as Kafka found himself thinking of Captain Nemo and *A Journey Through Planetary Space* when he saw a revenue cutter on Lago Maggiore.

In Milan, where I had some strange adventures fifteen years ago, Max and Franz (one almost envisages them as a couple invented by Franz himself) decided to go on to Paris, since cholera had broken out in Italy. At a

Sonthofen

coffee-house table in the cathedral square, they discuss apparent death and shooting pains in the region of the heart – obviously a particular obsession in the now sclerotic Habsburg Empire which had been suspended in a kind of afterlife for decades. Mahler, notes Kafka, had expected those pains in the heart too. He had died only a few months earlier at the Löw Sanatorium on 18 May as a thunderstorm broke over the town, just as there was a thunderstorm on the day of Beethoven's death.

Open in front of me now I have a recently published album containing photographs of Mahler. He is sitting on the deck of an ocean-going liner, walking in the countryside near his house in Toblach, on the beach in Zandvoort, asking a passer-by the way in Rome. He looks to me very small, rather like the impresario of a touring theatrical company down on its luck. In fact the passages of his music I like best are those where you can still hear the Jewish village musicians playing in the distance. Not so long ago I was listening to some Lithuanian buskers in the pedestrian zone of a North German town, and their music sounded exactly the same. One had an accordion, another a battered tuba, the third a double bass. As I listened, hardly able to tear myself away, I understood why Wiesengrund once wrote of Mahler that his music was the cardiogram of a breaking heart.

The friends spend their few days in Paris in rather melancholy mood, going on several sight-seeing expeditions and searching for the joys of love in a 'rationally furnished' brothel with 'an electric bell', where the business was conducted so swiftly that you were out in the street again before you knew it. 'It is difficult,' writes Kafka, 'to see the girls there very closely . . . I really remember only the one who was standing straight in front of me. She had gaps in her teeth, stood very upright, held her dress together with her clenched fist over her pudenda, and rapidly opened and closed her large eyes and her large mouth. Her blonde hair was untidy. She was thin. Felt afraid of forgetting to keep my hat on. You positively have to wrench your hand away from the brim.' Even the brothel has its own social standards. 'A long, lonely, pointless way home,' the note concludes. Max returns to Prague on 14 September. Kafka spends another week in the sanatorium at the natural spa of Erlenbach in Zürich. 'Travelled with a Jewish goldsmith from Krakau,' he writes after arriving. Kafka must have met this young man, who had already travelled widely, on the way back from Paris to Zürich. He mentions that getting out of the train the goldsmith carries his small suitcase like a heavy burden. 'He has,' writes Kafka, 'long, curly hair through which he occasionally runs his fingers, a bright gleam in his eyes, a slightly hooked nose, hollow cheeks, a suit of American cut, a frayed shirt, socks falling down over his shoes.' A travelling journeyman – what had he been doing in Switzerland? Kafka, we are told, took another walk that first evening in the dark little garden of the sanatorium, and next day there were 'morning gymnastic exercises to the sound of a song from *Des Knaben Wunderhorn* played by someone on the cornet'.

Dream Textures

A brief note on Nabokov

At the very beginning of Nabokov's autobiography, pro-grammatically entitled *Speak, Memory*, there is the story of a man who, we must assume, is still very young, and who suffers a panic attack when he first sees a home movie shot in his parents' house a few weeks before his birth. All the images trembling on the screen are familiar to him, he recognizes everything, everything is right except for the fact, which disturbs him deeply, that he himself is not where he has always been, and the other people in the house do not seem to mourn his absence. The sight of his mother waving from one of the windows on the upper floor is felt by the distressed viewer to be a farewell gesture, and he is terrified by the sight of the new baby carriage standing on the porch – 'with the smug, encroaching air of a coffin; and even that was empty, as if, in the reverse course of events, his very bones had disintegrated'. Nabokov is here suggesting an experience of the anticipation of death in the memory of a time before life, something that makes the viewer a kind of ghost in his own family. Nabokov repeatedly tried, as he himself has said, to cast a little light into the darkness lying on both sides of our life, and thus to illuminate our incomprehensible existence. Few subjects therefore, to my mind, preoccupied him more than the study of spirits, of which his famous passion for moths and butterflies was probably only an offshoot. At any rate, the most brilliant passages in his prose often give the impression that our worldly doings are being observed by some other species not yet known to any system of taxonomy whose emissaries sometimes assume a guest role in the plays performed by the living. Just as they appear to us, so Nabokov conjectures, so we appear to them: fleeting, transparent beings of uncertain provenance and purpose. They are most commonly encountered in dreams, 'in surroundings they never visited during their earthly existence', and are 'silent, bothered, strangely depressed', obviously suffering severely from their exclusion from society, and for that reason, says Nabokov, 'they sit apart, staring at the floor, as if death were a dark taint, a shameful family secret'. Nabokov's speculations about those who tread the border between life and the world beyond originate in the world of his childhood, which vanished without trace in the October Revolution; despite the evocative accuracy of his memories, he sometimes wonders whether that Arcadian land ever really existed. Cut off irrevocably as he was from his place of origin by the decades of terror in Russian history, he must surely have felt that retrieving one of its images caused him severe phantom pains, even though he usually looks discreetly at what he has lost only through the prism of irony. In the fifth chapter of *Pnin* he speaks at length and in different voices of the price you must pay on going into exile: not least, beside the material goods of life, the certainty of your own reality. The young emigrants of the early novels, Ganin, Fyodor and Edelweiss, are already marked much more deeply by the experience of loss than by their new and foreign surroundings. Unexpectedly finding themselves on the wrong side of the frontier, they are airy beings living a quasi-extraterritorial, somehow unlawful afterlife in rented rooms and boarding houses, just as their author lived remote from the reality of Berlin in the twenties. The strange unreality of such an existence in a foreign land seems to me nowhere more clearly expressed than in Nabokov's remark, made in passing, that he had appeared as an extra in evening dress in several of the films shot in Berlin at that time, which frequently included doppelgangers and such shadowy figures among their characters. There is no proof anywhere else of these appearances of his, so we do not know whether any of them may still be faintly preserved on a brittle strip of celluloid or whether they are now all extinguished, and it seems to me that they have something of the ghostly quality to be found in Nabokov's own prose, for instance in *The Real Life of Sebastian Knight* in the passage where the narrator V., in conversation with Sebastian's student friend in Cambridge, has a feeling that the ghost of his brother, whose story is on his mind, is moving round the room in the light reflected from the fire on the hearth. This scene of course echoes the ghost stories that were so popular in the eighteenth and nineteenth centuries while a rational view of the world was making itself felt. Nabokov liked to make use of such clichés: dust swirls in circles above the floor, there are inexplicable draughts of air, curiously iridescent effects of light, mysterious coincidences and strange chance meetings. In the train to Strasbourg V. finds himself opposite a gentleman called Silbermann whose shape blurs to an indistinct outline in the evening light as the train goes on and on straight into the sunset. Silbermann is a commercial traveller by profession, one of those restless spirits who often cross the narrator's paths in Nabokov's books. Silbermann asks whether V. is a traveller too, and on getting an answer in the affirmative wants to know exactly what he travels in. V. tells him that he travels in the past, a remark that Silbermann instantly understands. Ghosts and writers meet in their concern for the past – their own and that of those who were once dear to them. As V. tries to trace the real life of Sebastian, that vanished knight of the night, he feels a growing suspicion that his brother is looking over his shoulder as he writes. Such intimations occur with striking regularity in Nabokov's work, perhaps because after the murder of his father and the death of his brother Sergey, who died of consumption in Hamburg in January 1945 while he was in a concentration camp, he had a vague sense of the continuing presence of those who had been violently torn from this life. As a result one of Nabokov's main narrative techniques is to introduce, through barely perceptible nuances and shifts of perspective, an invisible observer – an observer who seems to have a better view not only than the characters in the narrative but than the narrator and the author who guides the narrator's pen; it is a trick that allows Nabokov to see the world and himself in it from above. In fact his work contains many passages written from a kind of bird's-eye view. From a vantage point high above the road an old woman picking herbs sees two cyclists and a car approaching a bend from different directions. From even higher up, from the dusty blue of the sky, an aircraft pilot sees the whole course of the road and two villages lying twelve miles apart. And if we could mount even further up, where the air grows thinner and thinner, we might perhaps, says the narrator at this point, see the entire length of the mountain range and a distant city in another land – Berlin, for instance. This is to see the world through the eye of the crane, as the Dutch painters sometimes did in painting scenes like the Flight into Egypt, when they rose above the flat panorama surrounding them down on earth. In the same way writing, as Nabokov practised it, is raised on high by the hope that, given sufficient concentration, the landscapes of time that have already sunk below the horizon can be seen once again in a synoptic view. Nabokov also knew, better than most of his fellow writers, that the desire to suspend time can prove its worth only in the most precise re-evocation of things long overtaken by oblivion. The pattern on the bathroom floor at Vyra, the white steam rising above the tub at which the boy looks dreamily from his seat in the dimly lit lavatory, the curve of the door frame on which he leans his forehead – suddenly, with a few well-chosen words, the whole cosmos of childhood is conjured up before our eyes as if pulled out of a black top hat. A large oil lamp on an alabaster stand is moved through the darkness. It hovers gently in the air, and gently settles in its place. The white-gloved hand of a servant which is now the hand of memory sets it down in the middle of the round table. We are attending the séance staged by Nabokov, and strangely familiar characters and objects emerge surrounded by that *claritas* which has always, since St Thomas Aquinas, been regarded as the sign of a true epiphany. Even for Nabokov, recording such visionary moments was a very arduous business. A short sequence of words often needed hours of work before the rhythm was right, down to the last cadence, before the gravity of earth had been overcome and the author, now as it were disembodied himself, could reach the opposite bank across his precarious bridge of written characters. Where that undertaking succeeds, however, one is borne along by the current of lines sweeping on and on into a radiant realm which, like everything that is wonderful, has a touch of the surreal about it, and finally seems to stand on the threshold of the revelation of an absolute truth, 'dazzling', as we are told at the end of *The Real Life of Sebastian Knight*, 'in its splendour and at the same time almost homely in its perfect simplicity'. To set something so beautiful in motion, according to both Nabokov and the messianic theory of salvation, no gaudy show is necessary, only a tiny spiritual movement which releases the ideas that are shut inside our heads and always going around in circles, letting them out into a universe where, as in a good sentence, there is a place for everything and everything is in its place. Nabokov has compared the shifts to which the writer must resort in composing such a sentence to the moves of a game of chess, one in which the players themselves are chessmen in a game played by an invisible hand. A steamer moves slowly away from its anchorage off Sebastopol and out on the water. From the banks the sounds of the Bolshevik revolution still echo – shouting and salvos of gunfire. But on the ship's deck father and son face each other over a chessboard, already immersed in the looking-glass world of exile ruled by the White Queen where one easily becomes dizzy simply by living backwards. 'Life is a Chequerboard of Nights and Days / where Destiny with Men for Pieces plays: / Hither and thither moves, and mates, and slays, / And one by one back in the Closet lays.' Nabokov would certainly have subscribed to the notion of eternal movement expressed in these lines translated from the eleventh-century Persian poet by Edward Fitz-Gerald, one of his distant predecessors at Trinity College, Cambridge. It is not surprising that from the moment of his exile Nabokov never had a real home, not in his years in England or in Berlin, or in Ithaca where he famously lived only in rented accommodation and kept moving on. His final place of residence in Montreux, where he could see above every earthly obstacle from his front-of-the-circle seat on the top floor of the Palace Hotel and out into the sun setting above the lake, was surely his dearest and most appropriate home after the Vyra estate of his childhood, just as a visitor called Simona Marini, who went to see him on 3 February 1972, tells us that the cable railway, particularly the chairlift, was his favourite means of transport. 'I find it delightful and dreamlike in the best sense of the word to hover in the morning sunlight on this magical perch between the valley and the treeline, observing my shadow from above as, in a seated position – a ghostly butterfly net in its ghostly hand – it moves gently down the flowery slope like a scissor-cut seen sideways among the dancing alpines and fritillaries. One day,' adds Nabokov, 'yet subtler dream material will meet the butterfly hunter as he glides away upright over the mountains, borne aloft by a small rocket strapped to his back.' This image of an ascension into heaven with its final touch of humour evokes another such passage, in my opinion the finest he ever wrote. It is at the end of the first chapter of *Speak, Memory*, and is an account of a scene that often took place at Vyra when the peasants from the village came up to the manor house with some petition or other, usually at midday when the Nabokovs were in their first-floor dining room. Once the lord of the manor Vladimir Dimitrievich had risen from table and gone out to see the petitioners and hear their request, then if the matter could be settled to the delegation's satisfaction it was their custom to throw him into the air three times by their united powers and catch him again as he came down. 'From my place at table,' writes Nabokov,

I would suddenly see through one of the west windows a marvellous case of levitation. There, for an instant, the figure of my father in his wind-rippled white summer suit would be displayed, gloriously sprawling in mid-air, his limbs in a curiously casual attitude, his handsome, imperturbable features turned to the sky. Thrice, to the mighty heave-ho of his invisible tossers, he would fly up in this fashion, and the second time he would go higher than the first and then there he would be, on his last and loftiest flight, reclining, as if for good, against the cobalt blue of the summer noon, like one of those paradisiac personages who comfortably soar, with such a wealth of folds in their garments, on the vaulted ceiling of a church while below, one by one, the wax tapers in mortal hands light up to make a swarm of minute flames in the mist of incense, and the priest chants of eternal repose, and funeral lilies conceal the face of whoever lies there, among the swimming lights, in the open coffin.

Kafka Goes to the Movies

Films, far more than books, have a way of disappearing not just from the market but from memory, never to be seen again. But one remembers some of them even decades later, and one of these rare exceptions, in my mind, is a ballad in black and white about two men neither of whom really knows where he is going. I saw it in a Munich cinema in May 1976, and afterwards, moved as one easily is by such experiences, I walked home through the mild night to my one-room flat in the Olympiapark.

Bruno Winter, I think, was the name of the man in dungarees, the character in this story directed by Wim Wenders who is on his way through the infinitely tedious region behind the front line of the Western world of the time. Viewers see him going from place to place, all of them disfigured by panels of man-made materials. He stops off at cinemas where almost no one goes any more. Bruno's life on the outskirts of a blinkered society was meant as a tribute to the springtime of the movies when the public gazed entranced at quivering strips of celluloid; it was both an obituary for a vanished form of entertainment and a look back at the years after the last war, when many of the more remote parts of the German provinces had visits from such entrepreneurs travelling around with movies. We ourselves, in W. on the northern borders of the Alps, could go to a weekly film show in the hall of the local inn, the Engelwirt, and see films like *The Secret Agent*, *The Man in Grey*, *Gilda* and *Geronimo*, with Lauren Bacall, Rita Hayworth, Stewart Granger, Chief Thundercloud and other stars of the past on screen.

But that is not my subject here; I am concerned with the other man who races up in a Volkswagen at the beginning of ['Kings of the Road'] *Im Lauf der Zeit*, when Bruno is shaving in the open air, and drives it intentionally (so much is instantly obvious) into the river by which Bruno has parked overnight. Bruno is not a little surprised. For a long moment the Beetle soars through the air as if it had learned to fly. To this day I remember the sight. As far as I recollect Robert Lander, the man at the wheel who rises from the ground in this spectacular manner, like his near namesake who was carried away by an umbrella, is a paediatrician or a psychologist, and after this unusual opening, which Wenders presents in matter-of-fact style, they travel together through the more remote regions of their native land having various

adventures, of which I remember most clearly a motor-
bike ride along an empty road, a very beautiful and
almost weightless sequence. Bruno is riding the bike, if
I remember correctly; and Robert sits in the sidecar
wearing the kind of sunglasses one used to have to put
on when being X-rayed. But to come to the real point:
it is this Robert (the actor's real name is Hanns Zischler),
shown in the film relishing the speed of the ride and the
ever-changing patterns of light and shade, who has just
published a book about Franz Kafka and what can be
discovered or conjectured about his interest in the art
of the cinema, still very new in his time.*

No author has had more written about him than Kafka.
Thousands of books and articles about his character and
work have accumulated within the comparatively short
space of half a century. Anyone with even an approxi-
mate idea of the extent and parasitic nature of this
proliferation of words may be forgiven for wondering
whether any further additions to this already excessively
long list of titles are needed. However, *Kafka Goes to the
Movies* is in a category of its own. Unlike the general
run of German critics whose plodding studies regularly
become a travesty of scholarship, and unlike the manufacturers of literary theory applying their astute minds
to the difficulty of Kafka, Hanns Zischler confines himself

Kafka geht ins Kino, Hanns Zischler (1996); English version, *Kafka
Goes to the Movies*, trans. Susan Gillespie (Chicago, 2003).

to a restrained commentary which never tries to go beyond its particular subject. It is this restraint, keeping to the facts alone and refusing to indulge in attempts at elucidation, that we can now see, looking back, distinguishes the best of Kafka scholars. Today, if you pick up one of the many Kafka studies to have appeared since the 1950s, it is almost incredible to observe how much dust and mould have already accumulated on these secondary works, inspired as they are by the theories of existentialism, theology, psychoanalysis, structuralism, poststructuralism, reception aesthetics or system criticism, and how unrewarding is the redundant verbiage on every page. Now and then, of course, you do find something different, for the conscientious and patient work of editors and factual commentators is in marked contrast to the chaff ground out in the mills of academia. To me at least – and I cannot claim to be entirely innocent of the fatal inclination to speculate about meanings – it seems increasingly that Malcolm Pasley, Klaus Wagenbach, Hartmut Binder, Walter Müller Seidel, Christoph Stölzl, Anthony Northey and Ritchie Robertson, all of whom have concentrated mainly on reconstructing a portrait of the author in his own time, have made a greater contribution to elucidating the texts than those exegists who dig around in them unscrupulously and often shamelessly. And among the faithful advocates we may now count Zischler, who was working on a television film about Kafka in 1978 when he first came upon the notes on the cinema scattered through the diaries and books, some of them, as Zischler says, very curt and cryptic. He was then surprised to find how little scholars had to say about them. Zischler saw this odd lack of interest as the occasion for an investigation he has carried out in true detective spirit in the intervening years, in Berlin and Munich, Prague and Paris, Copenhagen and Verona, and he has now collected the results in a volume of surprising finds, unpretentiously written and exemplary in every way.

Overwhelmed with visual stimulation as we are today, it is difficult for us to understand the fascination that movie images exerted in Kafka's time on audiences ready to abandon themselves to the illusion of an art which in many respects was still primitive, and was considered inferior by the arbiters of good taste. But Zischler, perhaps because he has been in front of the camera lens himself, knows all about the curiously mingled sense of identification and alienation felt when – in the extreme case, but it is a frequent one in the cinema – you can see yourself die. To Kafka, who was always yearning for his own dissolution, to perish almost imperceptibly in fugitive images running inexorably away like life itself must have been like the temptation of St Anthony in the desert. According to his own account and those of others, his eyes more than once filled with tears at the sight of such scenes in the movie theatre. Which scenes we do not know, but he may well have felt like Peter Altenberg, who resembled him in many ways and defended the cinema, an art despised by the 'psychological clowns of literature', with the following reminiscence, quoted by Zischler: 'My tender fifteen-year-old girlfriend and I, a fifty-two-year-old, cried hot tears over the nature sketch *Under the Starry Sky*, in which a poor French canal boat-hauler pulls his dead fiancée upstream, slowly and with difficulty, through blooming fields.' Kafka could surely have shed tears too over the French boat-hauler and his lifeless fiancée, for the picture would have suggested so much to him: the torment of a never-ending labour like some mythical punishment, mankind out of place in natural surroundings, the story of an unhappy engagement, untimely death. 'Dearest,' he writes to Felice about a photograph from which she looked at him with a melancholy expression, 'pictures are beautiful, we cannot do without pictures, but they torment us too.'

We are so moved by photographic images because of the curious aura of another world that sometimes emanates from them. Kafka, as many of his diary notes show, could fix such pictures in the mental snapshots he took with his sympathetic but ice-cold eye. Of Frau Tschissik, the Jewish actress, he makes a particular note about 'her hair set in 2 waves and illuminated by the gaslight', and a little later, in his description of the same woman, he comes to her cosmetics. 'I usually hate the use of powder,' he writes, 'but if this whiteness, like a veil clinging close to the skin and of a slightly cloudy, milky colour is the effect of powder, then all women should powder themselves.' In passages like these and many others, where the observer who stands a great distance away, yet is consumed by longing, is absorbed in the individual, isolated aspects of a physicality beyond his reach, for instance the 'faint white of the low neck of a blouse', we may conjecture that the erotic aura of such pictures – snapshots taken, so to speak, without permission – is due to their proximity to death. For the very reason that looking at one's fellow men with so pitiless a gaze is forbidden, one has to look again and again. The all-revealing, all-penetrating gaze is subject to compulsive repetition, always wanting to reassure itself that it really did see what it saw. Nothing is left but looking, an obsession in which real time is suspended while, as we sometimes feel in dreams, the dead, the living and the still unborn come together on the same plane. When Kafka visits the Kaiser Panorama in Friedland on a business trip in the winter of 1911, and looks through the eyepiece into the depths of artificial space, he sees the city of Verona populated by people 'like wax figures, their soles fixed to the ground on the sidewalk'. Two years later he will be walking in those very streets and feeling as remote from everything living as the wax figures he saw in Friedland. The innermost mystery of secular metaphysics is this strange sensation of physical absence, something evoked by what might be called an over-developed gaze. Significantly, the customers coming out of the twilight of the peepshow and going back into the street always have to give themselves a little shake before they are fully in control of the bodies they had shed as they were absorbed in looking at the panorama.

Kafka's comments on photography suggest that he felt there was something fundamentally uncanny about this way of copying life. Friedrich Thieberger, for instance, remembers once meeting Kafka in the street when he himself had an unwieldy box for making photographic enlargements under his arm. Thieberger writes that Kafka asked, in surprise, 'Taking photographs?' adding, 'That's really rather sinister.' Then, after a short pause, he continued, 'And you enlarge them as well!' Kafka's books too contain many indications of the vague horror he felt at the impending mutations of mankind as the age of technical reproduction opened, mutations in which he probably saw the imminent end of the autonomous individuality formed by bourgeois culture. The freedom of movement of the heroes of his novels and stories, which is not great to begin with, steadily undergoes further restrictions in the course of the action, while figures already called to life by an inscrutable series of laws take over, characters such as the court functionaries, the two idiotic assistants and the three lodgers in *The Metamorphosis*, executives and officials whose purely functional, amoral nature is obviously better suited to this new state of affairs. In the Romantic period the doppelganger which first aroused a fear of mechanical appliances was still a haunting and exceptional phenomenon; now it is everywhere. The whole technique of photographic copying ultimately depends on the principle of making a perfect duplicate of the original, of potentially infinite copying. You had only to pick up a stereoscopic card and you could see everything twice. And because the copy lasted long after what it had copied was gone, there was an uneasy suspicion that the original, whether it was human or a natural scene, was less authentic than the copy, that the copy was eroding the original, in the same way as a man meeting his doppelganger is said to feel his real self destroyed.

For such reasons I have always wanted to know whether Kafka ever saw the film *The Student of Prague*, large parts of which were shot in his native city in 1913; it must certainly have been screened there too. It is true that there is no reference to it anywhere in Kafka's letters and diaries, and Zischler tells us nothing about it either, but we may assume that the people of Prague did not ignore this famous product of the new cinematic art, with its brightly lit exterior shots. Supposing that Kafka really did see the film at this time, it would have been almost inevitable for him to recognize his own story in that of the student Balduin who is pursued by his own likeness, just as in the same year his reflections on a still from the film with Albert Bassermann, *Der Andere* ['The Other'], on which Zischler does write at some length, led to Kafka's producing what Zischler calls 'a snapshot of himself'. The still, which Kafka describes to Felice, reminds him of a production of *Hamlet* that he saw in Berlin, and of a part of his life that is now behind him, a kind of legacy in which, as so often happens when one is looking at old photographs, he is horrified to become aware of the progressive de-realization of his own person and the approach of death. Ghostly is perhaps the best word to describe Bassermann's appearance here. Indeed, early movies are ghostly in general, and not just because their favourite subjects included split personalities, doppelgangers and revenants, extrasensory perception and other parapsychological phenomena, but also because of the way that for technical reasons the actors moved in and out of what was still the completely motionless scene around them like ghosts walking through a wall. Most ghostly of all, of course, is the quasi-transcendental gaze cultivated by the male stage actors of the time which found its ultimate expression in film, a gaze that seems to be bent on a life in which the tragic hero no longer has any part. Kafka, who often felt like a ghost among his fellow men, knew of the insatiable greed felt by the dead for those who are still alive. All his writing can be understood as a form of noctambulism, or the stage preceding it. 'Walked in the streets for two hours weightless, boneless, bodiless, and thought of what I have been through while writing this afternoon,' he notes once. He imagines sending nocturnal letters to Berlin, and he himself is the phantom who, he tells Milena, drinks the kisses that he has sent out of the air before they can arrive. Zischler also quotes the passage from a letter where Kafka tells us how, going home in the electric tram, he read fragments of the posters he passed, concentrating hard. Zischler comments that Kafka's curiosity made him soak up such images. They were obviously his substitute for a life that he could not have, insubstantial nourishment from which he was constantly developing fantastic scenarios in his dreams, both sleeping and waking, repeatedly becoming a bizarre figure from the movies himself in those scenarios. There was a strange episode when, so he tells Max Brod on a postcard, he felt faint at the doctor's, had to lie down on the couch, and suddenly 'felt so very much a girl that I attempted to put my girl's skirt in order with my fingers'. Are not such dream sequences like films screened in the camera obscura of his mind, through which he moves like his own ghost? Zischler delicately probes the currents running between reality and imagination. The films about which he writes are really just the filter through which a new light is cast on the intensity of an almost uninterrupted process of dreaming and mourning, shifting between real life and fiction. Kafka's diaries are full of accounts of experiences in which daily life dissolves into airy pictures before our eyes, as if in a cinematic effect. For instance, he stands on a railway station platform, saying goodbye to the actress Frau Klug.

We . . . shook hands, I took off my hat and then held it to my chest, we stepped back as one does when a train is about to start, as if to show that all is over and one is reconciled to it. But the train did not start yet, and we approached each other again; I was glad of that, she asked after my sisters. All of a sudden the train slowly began to move, Frau Klug got her handkerchief ready to wave, called that I must write to her, did I have her address, she was already too far off for me to be able to reply in words, I pointed to Löwy from whom I could get her address, good, she nodded quickly to me and to him and waved her handkerchief, I raised my hat, clumsily at first, with more ease the further away she was. Later I remembered my impression that the train was not really moving away but only going the short distance through the station to act a scene for us and then disappear. When I was half asleep that same evening Frau Klug appeared to me, unnaturally small, almost without legs, wringing her hands with a despairing expression, as if some great misfortune had befallen her.

The drama of a whole life is contained in this diary note, the events cut like a film – unrequited love, the pain of parting, a lapsing into death, the return of a woman cheated of her happiness.

The shift into fantasy so characteristic of Kafka's writing, also found as something to be taken for granted in the passage just quoted, has often tended to obscure the fact that the author's apparently hopelessly eccentric consciousness in fact closely reflected the social problems of his time. Nowhere is this clearer than in Kafka's concern with the Jewishness that was lost to him. Characteristically, academic German literary criticism, particularly in Germany, showed very little understanding until the 1980s of a subject that was obviously of prime importance to Kafka himself. Even today the critics have not really compensated for this deficiency, which is due to an almost wilful lack of understanding, and consequently Zischler's study of Kafka's diary entry of 23 October 1921 is particularly interesting. 'Afternoon, Palestine film,' writes Kafka, without further comment. Zischler explains that this film, which bore the title *Shivat Zion*, was a documentary made in Jerusalem about the building of Jewish Palestine by the pioneers there, shown by the Zionist *Selbstwehr* ['Self-Defence'] organization at a time when more and more Jews were thinking of emigrating because even then their situation was becoming increasingly difficult; it must, he says, have made a lasting impression on many of the Prague Jews who went to the private screening at the Lido-Bio cinema. Afterwards, Zischler tells us, a film of the Eleventh Zionist Congress and Gymnastic Exhibition in Karlsbad was shown. It is not clear whether the gymnastic competition was a Jewish one, but that is not out of the question, for the realization of the Zionist utopia was primarily linked with an appeal to youth, and ideas of the physical training and physiological regeneration of the people were very much to the fore, as indeed they had been since the early nineteenth century in the emergent nationalist German ideology from which Zionism always took its cue. In the image of themselves that they projected, the two peoples, awakening from long oppression or rousing themselves from alleged neglect, were almost exactly the same, even if their standards and ambitions were different.

A reporter for the *Selbstwehr* journal, quoted by Zischler, describes how the Sunday morning habitués of the Lido-Bio had to wait until the first showing of the Palestine film was over; it began at eight-thirty in the morning. 'More and more salvos of applause are heard from the interior of the hall,' he writes, adding that a woman who had taken a look at the screen inside told the other people waiting, 'You hardly want to believe they are Jews, they don't look like it at all, I don't know, but their blood must have changed.' This story reminded me of another which, like my experience of the flying Robert in the movie, dates from the year

1976. I had been to a performance of Lessing's *Nathan the Wise* at the Coburg Landestheater, against my real inclinations because I dislike both the continuing misuse of this play, which I regard as rather questionable anyway, and German theatrical culture in general. At any rate, when what turned out to be an unspeakable performance was over and I was on my way out I heard an elderly lady, who must have been in full possession of her senses during the 'great days' of the German people, telling her friend in a confidential whisper: 'Well, he certainly played Nathan well. You might have thought he was a real Jew.' So unfathomable is this utterance that anyone who contemplates it must surely be overcome by vertigo, as indeed one is before most of the manifestations of the German–Jewish symbiosis. The overriding concept of those mirror-image identities is the myth of the Chosen People, to which the Germans blindly subscribed at the time when their ideas of national emancipation were taking a wrong turn. Whereas Herzl may still have been trying to square the circle when he suggested that German would be the language spoken in Zion, Hitler (somewhere in his table talk, I think) came to a conclusion which he thought irrefutably justified the annihilation of the Jews: there could not be two Chosen Peoples.

The 'Palestine film' was the last of Kafka's visits to the cinema mentioned in Zischler's book. What Kafka thought of the film we do not know, either from him or from any other source. All that is certain is that he did not go to the cinema very often afterwards. At least he was spared *Triumph of the Will*, though we may wonder what he would have thought if he had been obliged to watch all that marching. Let me be allowed one more discursion. According to Zischler, on 20 September 1913, the day when Kafka, in a state of long-term depression, felt the tears come to his eyes in a movie theatre in Verona, the films *Poveri bambini*, *Il celebro bandito Garouche* and *La lezione dell'abisso* were showing in the cinemas of that city. *La lezione dell'abisso* ['The Lesson of the Abyss'] was the precursor of the heroic Alpine genre in which Leni Riefenstahl made her name two decades later. In 1935 Riefenstahl – who I am told is still swimming and diving in the blue waters of the Maldives – was shooting a film high among the snow-white, cloud-capped mountains of Bavaria. There is nothing visible but the sky, while the Führer, a numinous being who is never seen (the audience views everything as if with a divine eye hovering above the world) is in a plane approaching the city of the Meistersingers where the Reich party rally is being held. Soon afterwards he drives through the streets with a great retinue. Of the old, touching Germany that once came into Kafka's mind as he leafed through the *Gartenlaube* ['Garden Arbour', a family magazine], there is nothing to be seen for the sheer press of human beings – they stand shoulder to shoulder everywhere beaming, standing on projecting vantage points, walls, stairs, balconies, hanging out of windows. The Führer's car moves through a positive torrent of people. And then, without warning, comes the strange, enormously evocative series of pictures in which, again looking down from high above, the audience sees a city of tents. There they are, stretching as far as the eye can see: white, pyramidal structures. At first, because of the unusual perspective, you do not see exactly what they are. Day is just dawning, and gradually, in the still twilit landscape, people come out of the tents alone or in twos and threes, all going the same way as if they had been called by name. The edifying effect is rather reduced when you see the men in close-up performing their morning ablutions bare-chested, a frequent emblem of National Socialist hygiene. Nonetheless, a magical picture of those white tents lingers in the mind. A people travelling through the desert. The Promised Land appears on the horizon. They will reach it together. But eight or nine years after this vision was recorded on film we shall have, instead, the black ruins of Nuremberg, the city where Zischler was born in 1947 when it still lay in rubble and ashes.

Kafka himself is known to have distrusted all utopianism. Not long before his death he said that he had been exiled from Canaan for forty years, and even the community which he sometimes longed for was basically suspect to him; he wanted only to dissolve away by himself, as the water runs into the sea. Few people ever seem to have been as much alone as Kafka appears in the last pictures of him, to which we may add one extrapolated from them, so to speak, and painted by Jan Peter Tripp. It shows Kafka as he might have looked had he lived eleven or twelve years longer. That would have been in 1935. The Reich party rally would have been held, just as Riefenstahl's film shows it. The race laws would have come into force, and Kafka, if he had had his photograph taken again, would have looked at us as he does from Tripp's ghostly picture – from beyond the grave.

Scomber Scombrus, or the Common Mackerel

On pictures by Jan Peter Tripp

The two sails were billowing in the west wind, and we set a course to take our boat cutting through the tidal current against which the mackerel, well known to be the greediest of fish, like to swim. As day dawned we cast out our lines. Soon we could see the barrier of the chalk cliffs in the twilit distance, bordered on top by the narrow band of dark fields and woods, but it was some time after that before the rays of the sun shone through the slight waves and the mackerel showed themselves.

Crowding close together, apparently in ever-increasing numbers, they shot past just below the surface of the water. Their stiff, torpedo-shaped bodies, whose outstanding feature is an over-developed muscular system that considerably restricts their agility, drives them straight ahead all the time. It is almost impossible for them to rest, and they can approach a destination only by describing a wide arc. Where exactly they go, unlike those fish which have more settled habits, has

The Unwritten Commandment

long been and still is a mystery. Ehrenbaum writes that
in the oceans off the American and European coasts
there are regions covering many square miles, and going
fathoms down into the depths, where mackerel can be
found in thousands of millions at certain times of the
year, and they disappear from them again as suddenly as
they came. Now, however, they were shining and flashing all around us. In the blue of their backs, which has
an irregular dark brown stripe down it, purple and
greenish-gold spangles sparkled in an iridescent play

of colour. We had often noticed when we caught the fish that at the hour of their death, indeed as soon as they felt the mere touch of the strange, dry air, the iridescence quickly faded and was extinguished, fading to a leaden hue.

The strange name of the mackerel reminds us of their wonderful shimmering appearance in life, for Ehrenbaum tells us elsewhere that it derives from the Latin epithet *varius*, or to its diminutives *variolus*, *variellus*, *varellus*, meaning pied or flecked, and consequently the *petite vérole* or syphilis takes its name from them, the disease that was once most usually caught in houses where, in the French idiom, a *maquerelle* was the word for a madam. Very likely the connections between the life and death of men and mackerel are far more complex than we guess. Isn't there, I thought as I pulled in the first line, an engraving by Grandville showing half a dozen particularly cold-blooded fish decked out in starched shirt fronts, ties and evening dress, sitting at a table and eating one of their own kind, or what would be hardly less terrible one of *our* kind? Perhaps it is no coincidence that to dream of fish is said to mean death.

Yet the same fish is an emblem of fertility among many peoples. Scheftelowitz, for instance, claims that among the Jews of Tunisia it was the custom to sprinkle mackerel scales on the pillow at weddings or on the Sabbath eve, while the Viennese psychiatrist and anthro-

Endgame

pologist Aisenbruk, who emigrated to California, tells us in his unjustly neglected writings that the Tyroleans like to nail a fishtail to the parlour ceiling at Christmas.

The facts of the matter, of course, are different. None of us ultimately knows how he may end up on someone else's plate, or what mysteries are hidden in that other person's closed hand. Even if we turn to ichthyomancy and instruments for dissecting the mackerel, if we carefully take it apart and question the oracle of its entrails, we shall be unlikely to get an answer, for such things only look back at us blind and dumb – the grain in planed wood, the silver bracelet, the ageing skin, the broken eye – and tell us nothing of the fate of our own kind. These thoughts preoccupied me until late in the evening. We had long since returned from our fishing trip, were back on dry land and looking out again at the grey sea, when it seemed to me as if something triangular were gliding out there, visible only now and then among the waves. 'Perhaps it's someone still out sailing,' said my companion, and she added, 'or else the fin of that great fish we will never net passing us far out at sea.'

The Mystery of the
Red-brown Skin

An approach to Bruce Chatwin

It is not easy to think of a contemporary German writer who would have ventured as much from the first as that tireless traveller Bruce Chatwin, each of whose five books, remarkable by any standards, is set in a different part of the world. Nor could you find anyone in Germany, where the good average mind is typical and the art of biography is held in low esteem, who after the early death of such an author would have emulated Nicholas Shakespeare in tracking him down in the suburbs of Birmingham, in London, on the Welsh borders, the island of Crete and Mount Athos, in Prague, in Patagonia, Afghanistan, Australia and darkest Africa, to find witnesses who could speak of the man who passed them by like a comet.

Just as Chatwin himself ultimately remains an enigma, one never knows how to classify his books. All that is obvious is that their structure and intentions place them in no known genre. Inspired by a kind of avidity for the undiscovered, they move along a line where the points of demarcation are those strange manifestations and objects of which one cannot say whether they are real, or whether they are among the phantasms generated in our minds from time immemorial. Anthropological and mythological studies in the tradition of Lévi-Strauss's *Tristes Tropiques*, adventure stories looking back to our early childhood reading, collections of facts, dream books, regional novels, examples of lush exoticism, puritanical penance, sweeping baroque vision, self-denial and personal confession – they are all these things together. It probably does them most justice to see their promiscuity, which breaks the mould of the modernist concept, as a late flowering of those early traveller's tales going back to Marco Polo where reality is constantly entering the realm of the metaphysical and miraculous, and the way through the world is taken from the first with an eye fixed on the writer's own end.

One of Chatwin's favourite books was Gustave Flaubert's *Trois Contes*, in particular the story of St Julian, who must atone for the sins of bloodshed he has incurred by his passion for hunting on a long journey through the hottest and coldest zones on earth: his limbs freeze and almost drop off as he crosses the ice fields, and in the blazing sun of the deserts the hair on his head catches fire. I cannot read a page of this terrifying story, the product of its author's profoundly hysterical disposition, without seeing Chatwin as he was, an *ingénu* driven by a panic need for knowledge and love, still like an adolescent at the age of thirty.

Chatwin was born into a family of building contractors, architects, lawyers and button manufacturers who became firmly established in the upper middle class of Birmingham during the Victorian era but who also – how could it be otherwise under the auspices of high capitalism? – included among their numbers some soldiers of fortune, failures and even criminal offenders. His father Charles, who was called up into the Navy in 1940 and was based in Chatham, spent the war years at sea as captain of a destroyer and was only a visitor at home, so that the child and his mother spent the early period of his life mainly with grandparents and greatuncles and aunts, moving easily in an extended and quasi-matriarchal society which must have given him not so much a strict sense of family as a certain clan feeling, and his mother's or grandmothers' brothers would have featured as his male role models. One of these uncles, who was very fond of his sister's blue-eyed child, told the biographer that Bruce noticed everything from an early age and looked at it like a scholar. 'And I thought it important,' he added, 'that he should become articulate.'

Chatwin, according to Shakespeare's informant, did indeed develop extraordinary eloquence and imaginative power. Like every true storyteller who still has links with the oral tradition, he could conjure up a setting with his voice alone and populate that stage with characters partly real and partly invented, moving among them just as his china collector Utz moves among his Meissen figurines. Chatwin too, as the invisible impresario of all that is extravagant, wears – even when he is travelling in the desert – a theatrical robe like the housecoat that hangs in Utz's bathroom, a masterpiece of haute couture in quilted, peach-coloured silk with appliqué roses on the shoulders and ostrich feathers around the velvet collar.

As a pupil at Marlborough College, one of the best schools in the country, Chatwin had a not very illustrious career, and by his own admission shone only as an actor, particularly in female roles, for instance in plays by Noël Coward. The art of transformation that came naturally to him, a sense of being always on stage, an instinct for the gesture that would make an effect on the audience, for the bizarre and the scandalous, the terrible and the wonderful, all these were undoubtedly prerequisites of Chatwin's ability to write. Scarcely less important must have been his training at the London auction house of Sotheby's, where he gained access to the treasure chambers of the past and acquired an idea of the singularity of artefacts, the market value of art, the importance of craftsmanlike skill and the necessity of precise research energetically pursued.

But most important of all in Chatwin's development as a writer were surely those early moments of pure fascination when the boy crept into his grandmother Isobel's dining room and, looking past his own blurred reflection, marvelled at the jumble of curios arranged on the shelves of the glass-fronted mahogany cupboard, all of them from very distant lands. It could not even be said where some of them came from or what they had been for; apocryphal stories clung to others.

For instance, there was a scrap of reddish fur that was kept in a pill box, wrapped in tissue paper. Nicholas Shakespeare tells us that this surreal object was a wedding present to Bruce's grandmother from her cousin Charles Milward, a clergyman's son who, when chastised once too often, had run away from home and gone to sea. He was shipwrecked on the coast of Patagonia. While he was in Patagonia one of his extraordinary ventures was to join forces with a German gold-panner and blow up a cave in Puerto Natales, bringing to light the remains of a prehistoric animal, the giant sloth or mylodon. He did a flourishing trade later in various body parts of the extinct creature, but the piece of skin sent to Birmingham was a gift to his beloved cousin.

The locked glass-fronted cupboard with its mysterious contents became, Shakespeare writes, a central metaphor for both the content and the style of Chatwin's work, and the remnant of the extinct animal was his favourite object. 'Never in my life have I wanted any-thing as I wanted that piece of skin,' wrote Chatwin to Sunil Sethi.

That skin, I think, is the key, and sums up the longing that sent him on his first major expedition across the Atlantic Ocean and down through the whole American continent, all the way to the Tierra del Fuego at the other end of the world, where he really did think he found a tuft of sloth hair in the same cave. At least, his wife said that he brought something of the kind back from his journey. There is no mistaking the fetishistic character of the sloth relic. Entirely without value in itself, it inflamed and satisfied the lover's illicit fantasy.

Something of this fetishistic greed went into his mania for gathering and collecting, and then into turning the fragments he found into significant mementoes endowed with a wealth of meaning, reminding us of what we, as living beings, cannot reach. This is probably the deepest of the many layers of the writing process. The fact that Chatwin tended so much that way is the reason why his work was read far beyond the frontiers of Great Britain. The universality of his vision lies in the way his descrip-tions evoke the recurrent themes of our imagination – an account, for instance, of an extraterritorial region where a community of Welsh settlers who emigrated over a hundred years ago still sing their Calvinist hymns, and where, under an ice-grey sky, the wind constantly blowing through the thin grass stunts the trees and bends them to the east.

The story of the shipwrecked sailor Charles Milward immediately reminded me of Georges Perec's autobiographical study *W ou le souvenir d'enfance* ['W, or the memory of childhood'], a work full of the most terrible and painful sensations and phantom anxieties, which begins with the account of a mentally sick boy called Gaspard Winckler whose mother, a famous soprano, takes him on a voyage around the world, hoping to cure him, and who finally disappears somewhere off the Cape of the Eleven Thousand Virgins or in the Todos los Santos straits. The Gaspard Winckler story is itself the paradigm of a destroyed childhood, and not for nothing does the similarity of name conjure up the unfortunate Kaspar Hauser. Chatwin too saw his journeys to the ends of the earth as expeditions in search of a lost boy, and thought he might have found him, as if in a mirror, in Gaimán when he met the shy pianist Enrique Fernandez, who has since died of Aids (like Chatwin himself) at the age of forty.

The key myth, in any case, was always that piece of strange skin, a relic that, like all mortal remains devoutly preserved and put on show, has something perverse about it, and at the same time something pointing far beyond the realm of the secular. It is an item that, as in Balzac's novel *La Peau de chagrin*, grants even our most secret and shameful wishes, but shrinks a little with the bestowal of each desired object, so that the gratification of our amorous longing is intimately related to the death wish. In a television interview given by Chatwin not long before his death we see him already wasted to little more than the proverbial skin and bone, with eyes dreadfully widened, but talking with an innocent and unprecedented passion about his last fictional character, Utz the china collector of Prague. It is the most shattering epiphany of a writer that I know.

The reader who begins Balzac's novel about the wild ass's skin, which is also and perhaps primarily the skin of grief and suffering, will soon come upon the passage in which Rafael, still called merely 'the young unknown' at this point, enters the crumbling building several storeys high where he acquires the fateful talisman. In those dozen pages, in the description of the lumber piled high in the storehouse, Balzac uninhibitedly sets out his whole mania for reality and words before us in what amounts to an act of authorial prostitution, but at the same time he reveals insights in the depths of the dreaming imagination. In the fantastic storehouse, designed as a kind of casket containing the world and inhabited by a desiccated little man over a hundred years old, the writings of the geologist Cuvier are recommended to Rafael as true works of poetry. In reading them, says the assistant leading him through the galleries of the emporium, you will glide over the unlimited chasms of the past, raised aloft by his genius, and as you discover the fossils of antediluvian creatures stratum by stratum in the stone quarries of Montmartre and the shale of the Urals, your soul will shrink with dismay at the sight of the billions of years and millions of nations forgotten by the short memory of mankind.

Moments musicaux

In September 1996, on a walking tour on the island of Corsica, I happened to be sitting during my first rest day in a grassy clearing on the outskirts of the Aitone forest, which lies at high altitude. I looked across hollows and valleys, deep blue to almost black in their depths, and saw a semicircle of granite crags and peaks, many of them towering up to a height of 2,500 metres or more. To the west was a wall of cloud looming darker and darker, but as yet the air was so still that not a blade of grass stirred. An hour later, when I had reached Evisa just as the storm broke and had taken refuge in the Café des Sports there, I spent a long time looking through the open door at the torrential rain slanting down into the street. The only other guest was an old man already equipped for the winter months in a woollen jacket and an old army anorak.

His eyes, dimmed by cataract, which he tilted slightly towards the light as a blind man would, were of the same ice-grey as the pastis in his glass. It did not seem to me that he had noticed the woman of curiously theatrical appearance who passed by under her umbrella a little later, or the half-grown pig that was following her. He kept looking up all the time, and as he did so he turned the six-sided stem of his glass jerkily with the thumb and forefinger of his right hand, as regularly as if he had the clockwork of a watch inside his breast instead of a heart. The sound of a kind of Turkish death march came from a cassette recorder behind the bar, and now and then a high-pitched laryngeal male voice sang, reminding me of the first musical sounds I ever heard in my childhood.

For immediately after the war there was almost no music at all in the village of W. on the northern outskirts of the Alps, apart from occasional performances by the severely depleted yodellers' group and the solemn music of the wind band, itself now reduced to a few elderly instrumentalists, which played for processions going round the fields and on Corpus Christi Day. Neither we nor our neighbours had a gramophone at this time, and the new Grundig radio that Aunt Therés in New York bought us just before I began school in 1950, for the fabulous sum of 500 marks, was hardly ever switched on during the week, probably because it stood in the parlour and no one used the parlour on working days. Early on a Sunday morning, however, I would hear the

Rottachtal ensemble or other local musicians on the radio with their dulcimers and guitars, for my father, who came home only at weekends, had a particular liking for this kind of traditional Bavarian folk music, which to me has taken on in retrospect the character of something terrible which I know will pursue me to my grave. A few years ago, for instance, after spending a restless night in the Hotel Kaiserin Elisabeth in Starnberg, I was woken from the sleep into which I fell at last towards morning by a radio alarm broadcasting two such Rottachtal folk singers whom I could only imagine, judging from the sounds they produced from the radio's tinny interior, as deformed and infirm; they were performing one of their merry songs about martens and foxes and all kinds of other animals, with each of its many verses ending in a *Holadroo-yoohoo, holladree-yo*.

The ghostly impression made on me by the Rottachtal singers trapped inside the radio that Sunday morning, when all was overcast by dense mists rising from the lake, was reinforced in a most uncanny way a few days later after my return to England, when I was searching through a box full of old photographs in a junk shop near Bethnal Green underground station in the East End of London, and almost to my horror came upon one of those picture postcards produced by the International Postal Union around the turn of the century, showing a painted panorama of the Allgäu mountains in snow and in front of it the Oberstdorf folk dancers in their traditional costumes, adorned with embroidered sprigs of edelweiss, tufts of chamois hair, cockerel feathers, silver talers, stag's teeth and similar tribal emblems. On finding this card, which had no message written on the back and which must certainly have gone on a long journey, I really felt as if the ten costumed men and women of Oberstdorf had been lying in wait for me here in their dusty English exile, just to remind me that I would never be able to escape the early history of my native land, where costumes and tradition played a not insignificant part.

After we had moved in December 1952 from our home in W. to the small town of S. nineteen kilometres away, with the aid of the Alpenvogel removals van, my musical horizons were gradually extended. I listened to Bereyter, our teacher, who always took his clarinet with him in an old knee-length sock on our class outings, just like the philosopher Wittgenstein, and played a number of beautiful pieces and arching melodic phrases, although without knowing that they were from the works of Mozart or Brahms, or an opera by Vincenzo Bellini. Many years later, when by one of those mere coincidences that are really no such thing I switched on the car radio one night while driving home, I was just in time to hear the theme from the second movement of Brahms's Clarinet Quintet that Bereyter had so often played, and recognized it again after all the time that had passed. At that moment of recognition I felt touched by the sensation, so rare in our emotional lives, of almost complete weightlessness.

Such was the enthusiasm inspired in me by Bereyter that at the time, in the summer of 1953, I wanted to learn the clarinet myself. But we had no clarinet at home, only a zither, so I had to go twice a week past the long wall of the riflemen's barracks to Ostrach-strasse, where Kerner the music teacher lived in a little terraced house with a tiled roof and a dark, turbulent sawmill canal flowing little more than five or six metres behind it, a canal from whose waters drowned bodies had quite often been pulled, as I could never help remembering at the sight of it, the most recent being the body of a boy of six whose brother was in my class at school.

Kerner the music teacher, a rather gloomy and melan-choly man, had a daughter of my own age called Kathi, a child prodigy known even abroad who had appeared in Munich, Vienna, Milan and God knows where else. Whenever I came for my zither lesson she was out of sight behind a closed door, seated under her mama's supervision at the grand piano which filled the whole parlour. The mighty rise and fall of the cascading notes of the sonatas and concertos she was practising made their way into the cramped little cubby-hole of a study where I was toiling away on the zither, while Kerner sat beside me, impatiently tapping his ruler on the edge of the table when my fingering was wrong. Playing the zither was a torment to me, and the zither itself a kind of rack on which you twisted and turned in vain and which left your fingers crooked, even leaving aside the ridiculous nature of the little pieces written for the instrument.

Only once, and at the end, as it was to turn out, of my three years of zither lessons, did I willingly take the instrument I had come to hate out of its case, when my grandfather, whom I loved dearly, lay dying during the first *föhn* storm after the Siberian winter of 1956, and as he drowsed, half unconscious already, I played him the few pieces I did not loathe from the bottom of my heart, ending, as I still remember, with a slow *ländler* in C major, which even as I played it, or so it appears to me now, seemed to be very long-drawn-out and to go on in slow motion as if it would never end.

I do not think that at the time, aged twelve, I could have guessed something I read much later, in one of Sigmund Freud's studies unless I am much mistaken: an observation which immediately struck me as convincing, suggesting that the deepest secret of music is that it is a gesture warding off paranoia, and we make music to defend ourselves against being overwhelmed by the terrors of reality. But after that April day I refused to go to any more zither lessons or even to touch the instrument again.

Among those *moments musicaux* which were accompanied by a first shadow cast over the feelings and which I have never been able to put out of my mind is, as it happens, a silent scene. In the single-storey annexe of the half-ruined railway station of S., which was closed down after the war, Zobel the conductor of the choir gave music lessons twice a week late in the afternoon. Especially in the winter months, when everything around was already dark, I would often stop outside what had once been the little waiting room on my way home to watch the music master in the bright lamplight inside, a thin and rather crooked figure conducting the muted music that I could hardly hear through the double window, or bending over the shoulder of one of his pupils. Among them were two to whom I felt particularly drawn: Regina Tobler, who tilted her head so prettily against her viola as she played that I felt a strange tugging in the region of the heart, and Peter Buchner, moving his bow back and forth over the strings of his double bass with an expression of utter bliss. Peter, who was so long-sighted that he had to wear glasses which made his moss-coloured eyes look at least twice as large as they really were, wore the same buckskin breeches and green jacket all the year round. Since he had no proper case for his instrument, which was much mended with sticking-plaster, and anyway could not have carried such a case from the Tannach housing estate where he lived to the middle of town, he tied his double bass, usually covered with a piece of flower-patterned wax-cloth, to a little handcart with string, and fixed the axle of the cart to his bicycle carrier, so that Peter was to be seen several times a week before or after the evening music lesson cycling from the Tannach estate to the old railway station, or back from the old station to the Tannach estate, sitting curiously upright on the saddle, his Tyrolean hat worn sideways on his head and his rucksack over his shoulder with the bow of the double bass sticking out of it, pulling the rattling little handcart along behind him either up or down Grüntenstrasse.

Zobel, the music teacher and conductor of the choir, was also organist of the parish church of St Michael, from which he barely escaped with his life on Sunday 29 April 1945 when the tower suffered a direct hit during High Mass. For an hour, I was told, the music master wandered around among the bombs still exploding everywhere in the lower part of town and the falling buildings, until just as the all-clear sounded he entered the sickroom where his wife had been lying for months. He was covered from head to foot with plaster dust and looked like the spectre of the catastrophe that had befallen S.

A good decade later – the bells had long ago been

hung in the rebuilt tower again – I always climbed to the loft during Mass on Sunday to watch the music master playing the organ. As I remember, he once remarked to me there was something wrong with the singing of the congregation assembled down in the nave, and said you could always pick out the people who sang out of tune from all the others. Easily the loudest of the untuneful singers was a certain Adam Herz, said to be a runaway monk, who made a living as a cowman on his Uncle Anselm's farm.

Every Sunday, Adam Herz stood on the extreme right of the back row of pews, and thus beside the steps up to the organ loft, where the enclosure in which for centuries lepers were penned during divine service used to stand. With the fervour of a man driven mad by terrible grief of the soul, Herz bawled out the Catholic hymns, all of which he knew by heart. His face was turned up and wore an expression of torment, his chin was thrust forward and his eyes were closed. Summer and winter alike he wore a sturdy pair of hobnailed boots on his bare feet and a pair of working trousers that were covered with cow dung and scarcely reached his ankles, and even in the iciest weather neither shirt nor vest, but only an old overcoat, his bony chest covered with curly grey hair visible between its lapels – as it strikes me today, just like poor Barnabas's chest under his messenger's suit in *The Castle*.

The music master, who played the accompaniment to the usual couple of dozen hymns loudly sung by the congregation more or less half asleep, came back to his proper senses again only at the end of Mass, when he virtually swept the herd of the faithful out of the church door with the storm of music he unleashed in his improvisations on the organ. As he played there in the church, which was soon empty and thus twice as resonant, performing variations in the boldest, indeed most reckless manner on a theme from Haydn's *Creation*, a symphony of Bruckner or another of his favourite works, his slightly built upper body moved back and forth like a metronome, and his bright patent-leather shoes seemed to me to dance a positive *pas de deux* on the pedals independently of the rest of him. He pulled out stop after stop, until the waves of sound coming from the organ pipes threatened, as I sometimes feared, to bring down the structure of the world itself, and he reached the climax in a last extreme crashing of chords, whereupon the music master suddenly broke off with a curious rigidity that involuntarily came over him at that moment, listening for a little longer to the silence flooding back into the trembling air with a happy expression on his face.

If you went from the parish church up the former Ritter-von-Epp-Strasse towards the middle of the town of S. you passed the Ochsenwirt Inn, where the *Liedertafel* or singing society met to perform every Saturday in the festive hall which stood empty during the week. I remember that once, when everything was buried deep in snow, I was lured by the sounds, strange to me, coming from the Ochsenwirt into the soundless winter air, went into the hall, and there, all alone in the dim light, watched a rehearsal of the closing scene of the opera that, as I had already heard, was soon to be performed on the stage which still dated from before the First World War and seemed to me miles away at that rehearsal.

I did not know what an opera was at the time, nor could I imagine what it might have to do with the three figures in costume and the shining dagger held first by Zweng the distiller and then by Gschwendtner the upholsterer, finally passing to the tobacconist Bella Unsinn, but I could tell from the despairing, interwining voices that the scene unfolding before my eyes could only be a tragic one even before Franz Gschwendtner took his own life, and Bella next moment sank unconscious to the ground.

And how surprised I was to see this tragic closing scene, which until then I had almost entirely forgotten, in a London cinema thirty years later, performed incredibly enough in almost identical costumes. Klaus Kinski, with his yellow hair standing out from his head as if electrified, stares out of the background of the stalls in the Teatro Amazonas of Manaus at the point when the action of the opera, set in the sixteenth century among Spanish grandees and mountain brigands, is just reaching the last of its many turns of fortune. Silva, wrapped in a black cloak, has handed the dagger to Hernani, played by Caruso in a kind of maternity smock. Hernani plunges it into his breast, rises heroically once more to the upper registers of song, and then falls sideways at the feet of the inconsolable Elvira, or rather Sarah Bernhardt, who shortly before, in an unprecedented bravura achievement, has come down the stone steps of the castle with her wooden leg.

Her face made up to look as white as a sheet, and clad in a rather shabby grey-blue lace dress, the actress looked exactly like Bella Unsinn thirty years earlier on the stage of the Ochsenwirt, while Enrico Caruso, who Fitzcarraldo believes pointed to him in the last moment of his life, looked with his broad-brimmed brigand's hat, twirled moustache and purple tights just like Gschwendtner the upholsterer as I remembered him.

The closing sequence of the film *Fitzcarraldo* also had special associations for me. Amidst unspeakable difficulties, a path is cut through the jungle and the steamer is hauled by means of primitive winches over the mountain crest between the two rivers until finally, when the mad plan has been as good as realized, it rocks gently in the water again. On the night of the festivities, however, the Jívaros, wishing to take another route, cut the cable and the steamer goes racing out of control down to the valley, between the rocky walls of the Pongo des Muertas. Fitzcarraldo and his Dutch captain see nothing but disaster coming, while the Jívaros, gathered on deck, merely look ahead in silence, believing that it is not far now to the better country they long for.

And in fact the ship does miraculously escape the cataracts of death. Somewhat battered and out of shape, but with the elegance of a prima donna, it moves out of the dark jungle in a great arc on the river, which is radiant with bright light. This is the hour of salvation in which – another miracle – news comes of the arrival in Manaus of an Italian company with an opera by Bellini, and here they come in several boats, to climb aboard and begin to play and sing. Behind the Puritans' pointed hats rises the cardboard backdrop of the mountains, which the libretto assures us are near Southampton. Chubby-cheeked Indians blow the French horn more beautifully than angels, and Rodolfo and the crazed Elvira, who has regained her reason now that the plot has taken a happy turn, unite their voices in a duet raised by the separation of their bodies to a state of pure bliss, ending with the words *Benedici a tanto amore*. All this time the ship of fools is drifting down the silvery river, so Fitzcarraldo's dream of an opera in the middle of the wilderness at last comes true. He himself stands leaning on a red theatre seat smoking an enormous cigar, listening to the wonderful music and feeling the slight breeze of their passage on his brow.

I encountered *I Puritani* for the first time at the age of twenty-two, in the house of a colleague who was a Bellini enthusiast and lived in Fairfield Avenue in Manchester, not far from Palatine Road, where the young engineering student Ludwig Wittgenstein stayed in 1908. It was a day as fine as another more than twenty years later, when I was sitting in my garden with a bad headache after finishing a work about torture that had occupied me for some time, and I heard the same opera again through the open window, broadcast from Bregenz. I still remember my sensations as the painkillers gradually began to work, and I felt the music of Bellini mingling with their analgesic effect like a relief and a blessing. I could hardly take in the fact that in addition it came through the summery blue of the ether from Bregenz, for the Bregenz Festival was inextricably bound up in my memory with the Singspiel *Zar und Zimmermann*, always performed in the lakeside theatre there year after year without fail.

The Bregenz Festival and the clog dance had been one and the same thing in my mind as far back as I can remember. If you went from S. to Bregenz on the Alpenvogel bus, you were going there to see the clog dance. The clog dance, along with various pieces by the composer Flotow and the famous aria from the *Evangelimann*, used to be music that always came top in the Sunday request concert broadcast by Bavarian Radio; we regularly listened to it at home after the children's programme. Nothing could compete, except perhaps the Don Cossacks and the *Soldier on the Banks of the Volga*, or the chorus of captives from *Nabucco*.

I could not really account for the nature of this pot-pourri at the time, but today it seems to me that these dubious German preferences had something to do with the time when the sons of the fatherland were sent East. So dazzlingly bright were the vast Ukrainian cornfields, I read not long ago, that many of the German soldiers who passed through them in the summer of 1942 wore sunglasses or snow goggles to avoid damaging their eyes. When the 16th Panzer Division reached the Volga at Rynok north of Stalingrad on 23 August as the light was fading, they saw beyond the opposite bank a country of deep green woods and fields apparently stretching away to infinity. Some of them, we know, dreamed of settling here after the war; others may have sensed already that they would never return from that distant land.

Teure Heimat, wann seh' ich dich wieder ('Dear homeland, when shall I see you again') runs the opening of the

German version of the chorus *Va pensiero*, and in a way
it was code for the vague feeling, never to be uttered
aloud, that the Germans were the real victims of the
war. Only in the aftermath of the so-called reparations
did anyone think of giving the Hebrews their own rights,
for instance in a production of *Nabucco* at Bregenz in the
mid nineties, making the anonymous slaves into real
Jews in striped uniforms. Soon after the beginning of
that particular season I took part, as I still regret, in
one of the events in the framework programme of the
festival, and in addition to my fee was given two tickets
for the performance of *Nabucco* that evening. Holding
these tickets, I stood undecided outside the theatre until
the last of the spectators had disappeared through the
entrances: undecided because with every passing year I
find it increasingly impossible to mingle with an audience; undecided because I did not want to see the chorus
dressed in costume as concentration camp inmates; and
undecided because I saw a storm coming up behind the
Pfänder and unlike other visitors to the festival had not
thought of bringing an umbrella. As I stood there a
young lady came up to me, probably because I looked
like someone let down by his companion, and asked
whether by any chance I had a spare ticket. She had
come a long way, she said, and was disappointed to find
that there were no tickets available at the box office.
When I gave her my two tickets and wished her a

pleasant evening she thanked me, a little dismayed to find that I did not want to see the Bregenz performance of *Nabucco* with her, as she might well have expected.

Half an hour after missing this opportunity I was sitting on the balcony of my hotel room. Thunder rolled across the sky, the rain soon began pouring down and it suddenly turned very cold, which did not surprise me, for it had snowed the day before in the Upper Engadine even though it was midsummer. Now and then lightning flashed, briefly lighting up the alpine garden that covered the whole slope behind the hotel. It had been laid out in long years of work by a man called Josef Hoflehner, with whom I had struck up a conversation on the afternoon when I saw him working in his rockery. Josef Hoflehner, who must have been well over eighty, told me that during the last war he was a prisoner in a wood-cutting squad in Scotland, working in Inverness and all over the Highlands. He had been a schoolteacher by profession, he told me, first in Upper Austria and then in Vorarlberg. I don't remember what made me ask him where he had trained, but I remember he told me it was in Kundmanngasse in Vienna, in the same institution and at the same time as Wittgenstein. He called Wittgenstein a prickly character, but would say no more about him.

Before going to sleep that evening in Bregenz, I read the last pages of a biography of Verdi, and perhaps for that reason I dreamed of the way the people of Milan, when the maestro lay dying in January 1901, put down straw in the street outside his house to muffle the sound of the horses' hooves, so that he could pass away in peace. In my dream I saw the street in Milan covered with straw, and the carriages and cabs driving soundlessly up and down it. At the end of the street, however, which went uphill at a curiously steep angle, there was a deep black sky with lightning flashing over it, just like the sky Wittgenstein saw as a boy of six from the balcony of the family's summer house on the Hochreith.

An Attempt at Restitution*

I can still see us in the days before Christmas 1949 in our living room above the Engelwirt Inn in Wertach. My sister was eight at the time, I myself was five, and neither of us had yet really got accustomed to our father, who since he returned from a French POW camp in February 1947 had been employed in the local town of Sonthofen as a manager (as he put it), and was at home only from Saturday to midday on Sunday. In front of us, open on the table, lay the new Quelle mail-order catalogue, the first I ever saw, containing what seemed to me a fairy-tale assortment of wares, from which it was decided in the course of the evening and after long discussions, in which our father got his sensible way, to order a pair of camel-hair slippers with metal buckles for each of us children. I think zip fastenings were still quite rare at the time.

*The text of this essay was first delivered as a speech at the opening of a House of Literature in Stuttgart in 2001.

But in addition to the camel-hair slippers we ordered a card game called the 'Cities Quartet' based on pictures of the cities of Germany, and we often played it during the winter months either when our father was at home or when there was another visitor to make a fourth. Have you got Oldenburg, we asked, have you got Wuppertal, have you got Worms? I learned to read from these names, which I had never heard before. I remember that it was a long time before I could imagine anything about these cities – so different did they sound from the local place names of Kranzegg, Jungholz and Unterjoch – except the places shown on the cards in the game: the giant Roland, the Porta Nigra, Cologne Cathedral, the Crane Gate in Danzig, the fine houses around a large square in Breslau.

In fact in the Cities Quartet, as I reconstruct it from memory, Germany was still undivided – at the time of course I thought nothing of that – and not only undivided but intact, for the uniformly dark brown pictures of the cities, which gave me at an early age the idea of a dark fatherland, showed the cities of Germany without exception as they had been before the war: the intricate gables below the citadel of the Nürnberger Burg, the half-timbered houses of Brunswick, the Holsten Gate of the Old Town in Lübeck, the Zwinger and the Brühl Terraces.

The Cities Quartet marked not only the beginning of

my career as a reader but the start of my passion for geography, which emerged soon after I began school: a delight in topography that became increasingly compulsive as my life went on and to which I have devoted endless hours bending over atlases and brochures of every kind. Inspired by the Cities Quartet, I soon found Stuttgart on the map. I saw that compared with the other German cities it was not too far from us. But I could not imagine a journey to it, any more than I could think what the city itself might look like, for whenever I thought of Stuttgart all I could see was the picture of Stuttgart Central Station on one of the cards in the game, a bastion of natural stone designed by the architect Paul Bonatz before the First World War, as I later learned, and completed soon after it, a building that in its angular brutalist architecture already to some extent anticipated what was to come, perhaps even, if I may be permitted so fanciful a mental leap, anticipated the few lines written by an English schoolgirl of about fifteen (judging by the clumsy handwriting) on holiday in Stuttgart to a Mrs J. Winn in Saltburn in the county of Yorkshire on the back of a picture postcard, which came into my hands at the end of the 1960s in a Salvation Army junk shop in Manchester, and which shows three other tall buildings in Stuttgart and Bonatz's railway station, curiously enough from exactly the same viewpoint as in our long-lost German Cities Quartet game.

Betty, for such was the name of the girl spending the summer in Stuttgart, writes on 10 August 1939, barely three weeks before the outbreak of the Second World War – when my father was already approaching the Polish border in Slovakia with his convoy of trucks – Betty writes that the people in Stuttgart are very friendly, and she has 'been out tramping, sunbathing and sightseeing, to a German birthday party, to the pictures and to a festival of the Hitler Youth'.

I acquired this card, with the picture of the railway station and the message on the back, on one of my long walks through the city of Manchester, before I had ever been to Stuttgart myself. When I was growing up in the Allgäu in the post-war period you did not travel much, and if you did go for an outing now and then as the 'economic miracle' set in, it was by bus to the Tyrol, to Vorarlberg, or at most into Switzerland. There was no call for excursions to Stuttgart or any of the other cities that still looked so badly damaged, and so until I left my native land at the age of twenty-one it was still largely unknown territory to me, remote and with something not quite right about it.

It was May 1976 when I first got out of a train at Bonatz's station, for someone had told me that the painter Jan Peter Tripp, with whom I had been to school in Oberstdorf, was living in Reinsburgstrasse in Stuttgart. I remember that visit to him as a remarkable occasion, because with the admiration I immediately felt for Tripp's work it also occurred to me that I too would like to do something one day besides giving lectures and holding seminars. At the time Tripp gave me a present of one of his engravings, showing the mentally-ill senatorial president Daniel Paul Schreber with a spider in his skull – what can there be more terrible than the ideas always scurrying around our minds? – and much of what I have written later derives from this engraving, even in my method of procedure: in adhering to an exact historical perspective, in patiently engraving and linking together apparently disparate things in the manner of a still life.

I have kept asking myself since then what the invisible connections that determine our lives are, and how the threads run. What, for instance, links my visit to Reinsburgstrasse with the fact that in the years immediately after the war it contained a camp for so-called displaced persons, a place which was raided on 20 March 1946 by about a hundred and eighty Stuttgart police officers, in the course of which, although the raid discovered nothing but a black market trade in a few hen's eggs, several shots were fired and one of the camp inmates, who had only just been reunited with his wife and two children, lost his life?

Why can I not get such episodes out of my mind? Why, when I take the S-Bahn towards Stuttgart city centre, do I think every time we reach Feuersee station that the fires are still blazing above us, and since the terrors of the last war years, even though we have rebuilt our surroundings so wonderfully well, we have been living in a kind of underground zone? Why did it seem to the traveller on a winter night, coming from Möhringen and getting his first sight from the back of a taxi of the new administrative complex of the firm of Daimler, that the network of lights glittering in the darkness was like a constellation of stars spreading all over the world, so that these Stuttgart stars are visible not only in the cities of Europe, the boulevards of Beverly Hills and Buenos Aires, but wherever columns of trucks with their cargo of refugees move along the dusty roads, obviously never stopping, in the zones of devastation that are always spreading somewhere, in the Sudan, Kosovo, Eritrea or Afghanistan?

And how far is it from the point where we find ourselves today back to the late eighteenth century, when the hope that mankind could improve and learn was inscribed in handsomely formed letters in our philosophical firmament? At the time Stuttgart, nestling amidst vineyards and overgrown slopes, was a little place of some twenty thousand souls, some of whom, as I once read, lived on the top floors of the towers of the collegiate church. One of the sons of the country,

Friedrich Hölderlin,* proudly addresses this small, still sleepy little Stuttgart, where cattle were driven into the market place early in the morning to drink from the black marble fountains, as the princess of his native land, and asks her, as if he already guessed at the coming dark turn that history and his own life would take: 'Receive me kindly, stranger that I am.' Gradually an epoch of violence then unfolds, and with it comes personal misfortune. The giant strides of the Revolution, writes Hölderlin, present a monstrous spectacle. The French forces invade Germany. The Sambre-Maas army moves towards Frankfurt, where after heavy bombardment the utmost confusion reigns. With the Gontard household, Hölderlin has fled that city for Kassel by way of Fulda. On his return he is increasingly torn between his wishful imaginings and the real impossibility of his love, which transgresses against the class system. Yes, he sits for days on end with Susette in the garden cabinet or the arbour, but he feels the humiliating aspect of his position is all the more oppressive. So he must leave again. He has gone on so many walking tours in his life of barely thirty years, in the Rhone Mountains, the Harz, to the

*The famous poet Friedrich Hölderlin (1770–1843) grew up in Nörtingen near Stuttgart. He had an unhappy love affair with the wife of his employer, the banker J. F. Gontard, in whose house he was a tutor. Around 1802 he showed the first signs of psychological disturbance, and he spent most of the rest of his life suffering from mental illness. Much of his poetry celebrates the ideals of ancient Greece.

Knochenberg, to Halle and Leipzig, and now, after the Frankfurt fiasco, back to Nürtingen and Stuttgart.

Soon afterwards he sets off again to Hauptwil in Switzerland, accompanied by friends through the wintry Schönbuch to Tübingen, then alone up the rugged mountain and down the other side, on the lonely road to Sigmaringen. It is twelve hours' walk from there to the lake. A quiet journey across the water. The next year, after a brief stay with his family, he is on the road again through Colmar, Isenheim, Belfort, Besançon and Lyon, going west and south-west, passing through the lowlands of the upper Loire in mid January, crossing the dreaded heights of the Auvergne deep as they are in snow, going through storms and wilderness until he finally reaches Bordeaux. You will be happy here, Consul Meyer tells him on his arrival, but six months later, exhausted, distressed, eyes flickering and dressed like a beggar he is back in Stuttgart. *Receive me kindly, stranger that I am.* What exactly happened to him? Was it that he missed his love, could he not overcome his social disadvantage, had he after all seen too far ahead in his misfortune? Did he know that the fatherland would turn away from his vision of peace and beauty, that soon those like him would be watched and locked up, and there would be no place for him but the tower? *A quoi bon la littérature?*

Perhaps only to help us to remember, and teach us to understand that some strange connections cannot be explained by causal logic, for instance the connection between the former princely residence of Stuttgart, later an industrial city, and the French town of Tulle, which is built on seven hills – 'elle a des prétentions, cette ville', a lady living there wrote to me some time ago, 'that town has grand ideas of itself' – between Stuttgart, then, and Tulle in the Corrèze region through which Hölderlin passed on his way to Bordeaux, and where on 9 June 1944, exactly three weeks after I first saw the light of day in the Seefeld house in Wertach, and almost exactly a hundred and one years after Hölderlin's death, the entire male population of the town was driven together in the grounds of an armaments factory by the SS Das Reich division, intent on retribution. Ninety-nine of them, men of all ages, were hanged from the lamp-posts and balconies of the Souilhac quarter in the course of that dark day, which still overshadows the memories of the town of Tulle. The rest were deported to forced labour camps and extermination camps, to Natzweiler, Flossenbürg and Mauthausen, where many were worked to death in the stone quarries.

So what is literature good for? Am I, Hölderlin asked himself, to fare like the thousands who in their spring-time days lived in both foreboding and love, but were seized by the avenging Fates on a drunken day, secretly and silently betrayed, to do penance in the dark of an all too sober realm where wild confusion prevails in the treacherous light, where they count slow time in frost and drought, and man still praises immortality in sighs alone? The synoptic view across the barrier of death presented by the poet in these lines is both overshadowed and illuminated, however, by the memory of those to whom the greatest injustice was done There are many forms of writing; only in literature, however, can there be an attempt at restitution over and above the mere recital of facts and over and above scholarship. A place that is at the service of such a task is therefore very appropriate in Stuttgart, and I wish it and the city that harbours it well for the future.

Acceptance Speech to the Collegium of the German Academy*

Born as I was in the Allgäu in 1944, I did not for some time perceive or understand any of the destruction that was present at the beginning of my life. Now and then, as a child, I heard adults speak of a coup, but I had no idea what a coup was. The first glimmerings of our terrible past came to me, I believe, one night at the end of the 1940s when the sawmill in the Plätt burned down, and everyone ran out of the houses on the edge of town to stare at the sheaf of flames flaring high into the black night. Later, at school, more was made of the campaigns of Alexander the Great and Napoleon than of what then lay only fifteen years in the past. Even at university I learned almost nothing of recent German history. German studies in those years were a branch of scholarship stricken with almost premeditated blindness, and as Hebel would have said, rode a pale horse. For a whole

*This speech was delivered by W. G. Sebald on the occasion of his being made a member of the German Academy.

winter semester we spent a proseminar stirring *The Golden Pot*,* without once discussing the relation in which that strange story stands to the time immediately preceding its composition, to the fields of corpses outside Dresden and the hunger and epidemic disease in the city on the Elbe at that period. Only when I went to Switzerland in 1965, and a year later to England, did ideas of my native country begin to form from a distance in my head, and these ideas, in the thirty years and more that I have now lived abroad, have grown and multiplied. To me, the whole Republic has something curiously unreal about it, rather like a never-ending déjà vu. Only a guest in England, I still hover between feelings of familiarity and dislocation there too. Once I dreamed, and like Hebel I had my dream in Paris, that I was unmasked as a traitor to my country and a fraud. Not least because of such misgivings, my admission to the Academy is very welcome, and an unhoped-for form of justification.

*E. T. A. Hoffmann's *Der Goldne Topf* (1814).

Notes

Strangeness, Integration and Crisis: On Peter Handke's play *Kaspar*

1 Peter Handke, *Kaspar* (Frankfurt, 1969), p. 12; Eng. *Plays: 1, Kaspar*, trans. Michael Roloff (New York and London, 1969, 1972), p. 57.

2 Jakob Wassermann, *Caspar Hauser* (Frankfurt, 1968), p. 5; Eng. trans. Michael Hulse (Harmondsworth, 1992), p. 3.

3 Friedrich Nietzsche, *Unzeitgemässe Betrachtungen* (Stuttgart, 1964), p. 101; Eng. *Unmodern Observations*, ed. W. Arrowsmith (New Haven and London, 1990), p. 88.

4 Ibid., p. 109; Eng., p. 91.

5 *Caspar Hauser*, p. 16; Eng., p. 13.

6 Ibid.; Eng., p. 14.

7 See *Kaspar*, p. 99; Eng., p. 139. *Caspar Hauser*, p. 20; Eng., p. 18. Rudolf Bilz, *Studien über Angst und Schmerz – Paläoanthropologie*, vol. I, part 2 (Frankfurt, 1961), p. 278.

8 Franz Kafka, *Erzählungen* (Frankfurt, 1961), p. 158; Eng. *Stories 1904–1924*, trans. J. A. Underwood (New York, 1981), p. 222.

9 Hugo von Hofmannsthal, *Terzinen – Über die Vergänglichkeit* (Frankfurt, 1957), p. 16.

10 David Cooper, *Death of the Family* (London, 1971), p. 11.

11 Peter Handke, 'Die Dressur der Objekte' in *Ich bin ein Bewohner des Elfenbeinturms* (Frankfurt, 1972), p. 145.

12 Ibid., p. 144.

13 Ibid., p. 145.

14 Peter Handke, *Ritt über den Bodensee* (Frankfurt, 1972), p. 95;
    Eng. *Plays: 1, The Ride Across Lake Constance*, trans. Michael Roloff
    (London, 1973) p. 227.

15 See Robert Musil, *Der Mann ohne Eigenschaften* (Berlin, 1930),
    p. 496; Eng. *The Man Without Qualities*, trans. E. Wilkins and E.
    Kaiser (London, 1954), vol. II, p. 318.

16 *Kaspar*, p. 20; Eng., p. 64.

17 Ibid., p. 21; Eng., p. 65.

18 Lars Gustafsson, 'Die Maschinen' in *Utopien* (Munich, 1970), p. 39.

19 *Kaspar*, p. 50; Eng., pp. 93–4.

20 Ibid., pp. 75–6; Eng., pp. 117–18.

21 Ibid., p. 55; Eng., p. 99.

22 This and the two following quotations are from ibid., p. 56;
    Eng., p. 100.

23 Ibid., p. 57; Eng., p. 101.

24 This and the following quotation are from ibid., p. 58; Eng.,
    pp. 101, 102.

25 This and the following quotation are from ibid., p. 92; Eng.,
    p. 133.

26 Ibid., p. 31; Eng., p. 75.

27 This and the following quotation ibid., p. 93.

28 Ibid., pp. 100–101; Eng., p. 140.

29 From the introduction to the German version of David Cooper,
    Psychiatry and Anti-Psychiatry (London, 1967); Ger. *Psychiatrie und
    Antipsychiatrie* (Frankfurt, 1971), p. ii.

30 Peter Handke, *Wunschloses Unglück* (Frankfurt, 1974), p. 48; Eng. *A
    Sorrow Beyond Dreams*, trans. Ralph Manheim (London, 1976), p. 31.

31 Ernst Cassirer, *Sprache und Mythos*, Studien der Bibliothek War-
    burg (Leipzig and Berlin, 1925), p. 5; Eng. *Language and Myth*,
    trans. Susanne E. Langer (New York, 1946), pp. 6–7.

Between History and Natural History: On the literary description of total destruction

1 Heinrich Böll, *Hierzulande – Aufsätze zur Zeit* (Munich, 1963),
   p. 128.

2 Günter Eich, 1907–72, poet and playwright; Paul Celan (pseudonym of Paul Antschel), 1920–70, poet; Wolfgang Borchert,

1921–47, poet, actor, writer of plays and short stories; Hans Erich Nossack, 1901–77, novelist who wrote on the air raids of the Second World War in 'Der Untergang' – much quoted in the present work; Ernst Kreuder, 1903–72, journalist and novelist; Ilse Aichinger, b. 1921, novelist, writer of plays and short stories; Wolfdietrich Schnurre, 1920–89, novelist and literary critic; Hans Werner Richter, 1908–93, novelist; Walter Kolbenhoff (pseudonym of Walter Hoffmann), 1908–93, novelist; Rolf Schroers, 1919–81, writer; Elisabeth Langgässer, 1899–1950, poet, novelist and essayist; Karl Krolow, 1915–99, poet; Siegfried Lenz, b. 1926, novelist; Arno Schmidt, 1914–79, novelist, essayist and critic; Alfred Andersch, 1914–80, novelist and essayist; Walter Jens, b. 1923, novelist and essayist; Marie Luise von Kaschnitz, 1901–74, novelist and poet.

3 Heinrich Böll, *Frankfurter Vorlesungen* (Munich, 1968), p. 121.

4 Hans Erich Nossack, 'Er wurde zuletzt ganz durchsichtig – Erinnerungen an Hermann Kasack' in *Pseudoautobiographische Glossen* (Frankfurt, 1971), p. 50. The text was first published in Hamburg in 1966 in the *Jahrbuch der Freien Akademie der Künste*.

5 In the essay cited above (p. 50), Nossack speaks of its being an international success.

6 Hermann Kasack, *Die Stadt hinter dem Strom* (Frankfurt, 1978), p. 18.

7 Ibid., p. 10.

8 A term coined by Nossack; see 'Er wurde zuletzt ganz durchsichtig', p. 152.

9 Kasack, *Die Stadt hinter dem Strom*, p. 152.

10 Ibid.

11 Ibid., p. 154.

12 Ibid., p. 142.

13 Ibid., p. 314.

14 Ibid., p. 315. Arno Schmidt's prose work of 1949, *Leviathan oder die beste der Welten*, rests upon comparable juggling with contemporary reality. In this work the theory of the successive self-realization of a negative cosmic principle is presented with physical and philosophical sophistry.

15 See Nossack, 'Er wurde zuletzt ganz durchsichtig', p. 47: 'Real literature was a secret language at the time.'

16 *Die Stadt hinter dem Strom*, p. 348.

17 Hans Erich Nossack, 'Der Untergang' in *Interview mit dem Tode* (Frankfurt, 1972), pp. 209, 225.

18 Ibid., p. 233.

19 Ibid., p. 230.

20 Ibid., p. 229.

21 Ibid., p. 210.

22 Ibid., p. 209.

23 This quotation is from the autobiographical essay *Dies lebenlose Leben* ['This Lifeless Life'], in which Nossack describes his time under the Fascist regime. It refers to a former fellow student who took his own life in 1933 because he wanted to be among the victims.

24 See in particular Canetti's *Crowds and Power*, Weiss's *Abschied von den Eltern* ['Farewell to my Parents'] and Hildesheimer's *Tynset*.

25 Nossack, *Interview mit dem Tode*, p. 193. The 'classical' figure embodying this attitude is probably Pastor Helander, who dies with his boots on, in Alfred Andersch's novel *Sansibar oder der letzte Grund* ['Zanzibar, or The Last Reason'], dubious as that book is in many respects. *Pseudoautobiographische Glossen*, p. 21.

26 'Der Untergang' in *Interview mit dem Tode*, p. 254.

27 Ibid.

28 *Pseudoautobiographische Glossen*, p. 21.

29 Hans Erich Nossack, 'Bericht eines fremden Wesens über die Menschen' in *Interview mit dem Tode*, p. 8.

30 'Der Untergang' in *Interview mit dem Tode*, p. 204.

31 Ibid., pp. 205, 208.

32 Ibid., pp. 211–12.

33 Ibid., pp. 226–7.

34 *In Darkest Germany* (London, 1947). The book is a compilation of newspaper articles, letters and observations by Gollancz himself, and in its very lack of literary pretension it conveys a precise impression of the situation of the German population directly after the war. It includes a chapter entitled 'This Misery of Boots', which is devoted to the footwear of the post-war Germans, as well as photographs documenting about twenty pairs of these boots and shoes. The extremely battered items of footwear shown do indeed suggest a phenomenon of natural history, reminding the viewer of all the connotations of the term 'stout shoes' (*festes Schuhwerk*) for the Germans even later. It is almost a model of the

documentary linking of past and present as practised by Kluge. Gollancz was also one of the few people to speak up for the German people immediately after the war, just as he had previously been one of the few to point, at the earliest possible moment, to the murder of the Jews in the concentration camps and suggest practical counter-measures, without getting much response. (See *Let My People Go – Some practical proposals for dealing with Hitler's massacre of the Jews and an appeal to the British public*, London, 1943. An impressive historical study of this subject has now been published: T. Bower, *A Blind Eye to Murder*, London, 1981.)

35 See *Frankfurter Vorlesungen*, p. 82.

36 'Der Untergang' in *Interview mit dem Tode*, p. 216.

37 *Frankfurter Vorlesungen*, p. 83.

38 Nossack, *Interview mit dem Tode*, p. 243.

39 Alexander Kluge, *Neue Geschichten. Hefte 1–18, Unheimlichkeit der Zeit* (Frankfurt, 1977), p. 102.

40 Theodor W. Adorno, *Prismen* (Munich, 1963), p. 267; Eng. *Prisms*, trans. S. and S. Weber (London, 1967), p. 260.

41 Kasack, *Die Stadt hinter dem Strom*, p. 82.

42 Ibid., p. 22.

43 Nossack, *Interview mit dem Tode*, p. 217.

44 Elias Canetti, *Die gespaltene Zukunft* (Munich, 1972), p. 58.

45 *Interview mit dem Tode*, p. 219.

46 Ibid., pp. 248–9.

47 Ibid., p. 256.

48 Theodor W. Adorno, *Kierkegaard – Konstruktion des Ästhetischen* (Frankfurt, 1966), p. 253.

49 Nossack, *Interview mit dem Tode*, p. 245.

50 *The Odyssey*, XXII, 471–3, trans. Robert Fagles (New York, 1995).

51 Nossack, *Interview mit dem Tode*, p. 245.

52 *Neue Geschichten*, p. 9.

53 Ibid., pp. 83–4. The conclusions that the reader can draw from these 'statements' converge with the ideas published by Solly Zuckerman in his autobiography *From Apes to Warlords* (London, 1978). Lord Zuckerman was scientific adviser on air warfare strategy to the British government during the war, and with great personal commitment tried to dissuade High Command of the bomber forces under Air Marshal Arthur 'Bomber' Harris from

continuing with the strategy of wholesale destruction that went by the name of Operation Overlord. He backed, instead, a selective strategy aimed against the enemy's system of communications, which he was convinced would have brought the war to an end sooner and with far fewer victims, an opinion that, incidentally, coincides with the conjectures on this subject put forward by Speer in his memoirs. Lord Zuckerman writes: 'As we now know, bombing at about a hundred times the intensity of anything ever suffered by European cities during the Second World War at no moment broke the spirit of the people of Vietnam against whom the American forces were fighting between 1964 and 1973. In those nine years, seven million tons of bombs were dropped on South Vietnam (which received about half of the total), North Vietnam, Laos and Cambodia – three times the total tonnage of British, American and German bombs dropped on European soil in the Second World War.' (*From Apes to Warlords*, p. 148.) These observations bear out his thesis of the objective pointlessness of 'area bombing'. As Lord Zuckerman says in his book, once he had seen for himself after the war the effects of the air raids on German cities he agreed to write an account entitled 'The Natural History of Destruction' for the journal *Horizon*, edited by Cyril Connolly, but unfortunately this project was never carried out.

54 *Neue Geschichten*, p. 35.

55 Ibid., p. 37.

56 Ibid., p. 39.

57 Ibid., p. 49.

58 Ibid., p. 53.

59 See Robert Wolfgang Schnel, 'Wuppertal 1945' in *Vaterland, Muttersprache – Deutsche Schriftsteller und ihr Staat seit 1945*, ed. K. Wagenbach, W. Stephan and M. Krüger (Berlin, 1979), pp. 29–30, which quotes this comment by Brecht in a context that is relevant here.

60 See Stanislaw Lem, *Imaginäre Grösse* (Frankfurt, 1981), p. 74; Eng. *Imaginary Magnitude*, trans. Marc E. Heine (London, 1985).

61 *Neue Geschichten*, p. 59.

62 Ibid., pp. 63, 69.

63 Ibid., p. 79.

64 *Interview mit dem Tode*, p. 121.

65 See Andrew Bowie, 'Problems of Historical Understanding in the
    Modern Novel', dissertation (University of East Anglia, 1979), an
    outstanding work which studies Kluge in its closing chapter.
66 *Neue Geschichten*, pp. 38, 54.
67 'Problems of Historical Understanding', pp. 295–6.
68 *Neue Geschichten*, pp. 106–7.

Constructs of Mourning: Günter Grass and Wolfgang Hildesheimer

1   Alexander and Margarete Mitscherlich, *Die Unfähigkeit zu trauern*
    (Munich, 1967), p. 9.
2   An almost entirely dismantled and de-industrialized Germany
    such as the Morgenthau Plan envisaged would hardly have been
    in any state to rehabilitate itself, and Robert Burton's description
    of melancholy states where the land lies uncultivated, desolate,
    full of swamps, marshes, wildernesses and the like, where cities
    fall into decay, towns are depressed and poor, villages are
    deserted, and the population is dirty, ugly and uncivilized, would
    probably have been very relevant to Germany.
3   This and the following three quotations are from *Die Unfähigkeit
    zu trauern*, p. 35.
4   Hans Erich Nossack, *Pseudoautobiographische Glossen* (Frankfurt,
    1971).
5   Hans Erich Nossak, 'Der Untergang' in *Interview mit dem Tode*
    (Frankfurt, 1972), p. 249.
6   Act I, scene 2.
7   *Die Unfähigkeit zu trauern*, p. 47.
8   Ibid., p. 48.
9   Ibid., p. 56.
10 Ibid., p. 57.
11 Ibid., p. 28.
12 Heinrich Böll, *Frankfurter Vorlesungen* (Munich, 1968), p. 8.
13 Ibid., p. 9.
14 *Die Unfähigkeit zu trauern*, pp. 19, 18.
15 Günter Grass, *Tagebuch einer Schnecke* (Reinbek, 1974), p. 80;
    Eng. *From the Diary of a Snail*, trans. Ralph Manheim (London,
    1974), p. 112.

16 Ibid., p. 27; Eng., p. 34. Lichtenstein's book did not appear until 1973. In the foreword to his monograph Erwin Lichtenstein comments that Grass, in his own latest book, refers 'to accounts and news reports as well as much factual material that he had from me'. And he continues: 'The reader of this *Diary of a Snail* will find my information expressed in the chapters of Günter Grass's book tracing the final period of the history of the Jews in Danzig.' (E. Lichtenstein, *Die Juden der freien Stadt Danzig unter der Herrschaft des Nationalsozialismus*, Tübingen, 1973, p. viii.) We have here a clear indication that there had been no research by local historians into the fate of the Jewish communities on the German side, and that little had changed in the state of affairs deplored by Jean Paul as 'Christian neglect of the study of the Jews'.

17 Günter Grass, *Katz und Maus* (Reinbek, 1963), p. 35; Eng. *Cat and Mouse*, trans. Ralph Manheim (London, 1962).

18 'Rede auf Hermann Broch' in Elias Canetti, *Aufzeichnungen 1942–1948* (Munich, 1969), pp. 159–60. *Tagebuch einer Schnecke*, p. 153; Eng., p. 223.

19 Walter Benjamin, *Ursprung des deutschen Trauerspiels* (Frankfurt 1963), p. 166; Eng. *The Origin of German Tragic Drama*, trans. John Osborne (London, 1977), p. 152.

20 *Tagebuch einer Schnecke*, p. 155; Eng., p. 223.

21 Ibid., p. 81; not in Eng.

22 Heinrich Böll, *Der Zug war pünktlich* (Munich, 1972), p. 34; Eng. *The Train Was on Time*, trans. Leila Vennewitz (London, 1970), p. 28.

23 *Tagebuch einer Schnecke*, p. 155; Eng., p. 96.

24 Ibid., p. 70; Eng., p. 97.

25 Ibid., p. 37; Eng., p. 49.

26 See *From the Diary of a Snail*, where Grass tells his children: 'It's true: you're innocent. I, too, born almost late enough, am held to be free from guilt. Only if I wanted to forget, if you were unwilling to learn how it slowly happened, only then might words of one syllable catch up with us: words like guilt and shame; they, too, resolute snails, impossible to stop.' (*Tagebuch einer Schnecke*, p. 13; Eng., p. 13.) The most notable feature of this passage is the less than convincing logic of the last couple of lines.

27 Ibid., p. 130; Eng., p. 188.

28 Ibid., p. 189; Eng., p. 274.

29 Ibid., p. 203; Eng., p. 294.
30 Wolfgang Hildesheimer, *Tynset* (Frankfurt, 1965), p. 30.
31 Ibid., p. 39.
32 Ibid., p. 46.
33 Ibid., pp. 155–6.
34 Act I, scene 1.
35 See Franz Kafka, *Briefe an Felice* (Frankfurt, 1967), p. 283.
36 Quoted from F. P. Wilson, *Seventeenth-Century Prose* (Cambridge, 1960), p. 45.
37 Ibid., p. 27.
38 Sir Thomas Browne, *Hydriotaphia, Urne-Buriall, or A Brief Discourse of the Sepulchrall Urnes lately found in Norfolk* (London, 1658). Reprinted in *The Prose of Sir Thomas Browne* (New York and London, 1968), p. 281.
39 *Tynset*, p. 185.
40 See *Ursprung des deutschen Trauerspiels*, p. 164; Eng., p. 150.
41 *Hamlet*, Act IV, scene 5.
42 *Tynset*, p. 87.
43 Theodor W. Adorno, *Ästhetische Theorie* (Frankfurt, 1970), p. 66; Eng. *Aesthetic Theory*, trans. Robert Hullot-Kentor (London, 1997), pp. 39–40.
44 *Tynset*, p. 186.
45 Ibid., p. 79. *Hamlet*, Act I, scene 5.
46 *Tynset*, p. 265.
47 Ibid., p. 14.
48 Wolfgang Hildesheimer, 'Brief an Max über den Stand der Dinge und Anderes' in *Manuskripte. Zeitschrift für Literatur* 76 (1982), p. 44.
49 *Lucifers Königreich und Seelengejäidt: Oder Narrenhatz. In acht Theil Abgetheilet . . . Durch Aegidium Albertinum, Fürstl.: Durchl: in Bayrn Secretarium, zusammen getragen* (Munich, 1617), p. 411 (quoted by Benjamin in *Ursprung des deutschen Trauerspiels*, p. 156).

Sources

Prose

'A Little Excursion to Ajaccio' ['Kleine Exkursion nach Agaccio'],
Frankfurter Allgemeine Zeitung, 10 August 1996.

'Campo Santo', *Akzente* 1 (2003), pp. 3–14.

'The Alps in the Sea' ['Die Alpen im Meer'], *Literaturen* 1 (2001),
pp. 30–33.

'*La cour de l'ancienne école*' in Quint Buchholz, *BuchBilderBuch* ['Stories
about Pictures'] (Zürich, 1997), pp. 13–15.

Essays

'Strangeness, Integration and Crisis: On Peter Handke's play *Kaspar*'
['Fremdheit, Integration und Krise. Über Peter Handkes Stück
Kaspar'], *Literatur und Kritik* 10 (1975), pp. 152–8.

'Between History and Natural History: On the literary description of
total destruction' ['Zwischen Geschichte und Naturgeschichte.
Über die literarische Beschreibung totaler Zerstörung'], *Orbis lit-
terarum* 37 (1982), 4, pp. 345–66.

'Constructs of Mourning: Günter Grass and Wolfgang Hildesheimer'
['Konstruktionen der Trauer. Günter Grass und Wolfgang Hildesheimer'], *Deutschunterricht* 35 (1983), 5, pp. 32–46.

'*Des Häschens Kind, der kleine Has*: On the poet Ernst Herbeck's totem animal'
['Des Häschens Kind, der kleine Has. Über das Totemtier des Lyrikers
Ernst Herbeck'], *Frankfurter Allgemeine Zeitung*, 8 December 1992.

'To the Brothel by way of Switzerland: On Kafka's travel diaries' ['Via Schweiz ins Bordell. Zu den Reisetagebüchern Kafkas'], *Die Weltwoche*, 5 October 1995, p. 66.

'Dream Textures: A brief note on Nabokov' ['Traumtexturen. Kleine Anmerkung zu Nabokov'], *Die Zeitschrift der Kultur* 6 (1996), pp. 22–5.

'Kafka Goes to the Movies' ['Kafka im Kino'], *Frankfurter Rundschau*, 18 January 1997.

'*Scomber scombrus*, or the Common Mackerel: On pictures by Jan Peter Tripp' ['*Scomber scombrus* oder die gemeine Makrele. Zu Bildern von Jan Peter Tripp'], *Neue Zürcher Zeitung*, 23/24 September 2000.

'The Mystery of the Red-brown Skin: An approach to Bruce Chatwin' ['Das Geheimnis des rotbraunen Fells. Annäherung an Bruce Chatwin'], *Literaturen* 11 (2000), pp. 72–5.

'*Moments musicaux*', *Frankfurter Allgemeine Zeitung*, 7 July 2001.

'An Attempt at Restitution' ['Ein Versuch der Restitution'], *Stuttgarter Zeitung*, 18 November 2001.

'Acceptance Speech to the Collegium of the German Academy' ['Antrittsrede vor dem Kollegium der Deutschen Akademie'] in *Wie sie sich selber sehen*, ed. Michael Assmann (Göttingen, 1999), pp. 445–6.

Pictures

Quint Buchholz, *Die Befragung der Aussicht (III)* ['Questioning the View (III)'], pen and coloured ink drawing on paper, 1989.

Jan Peter Tripp, *Das ungeschriebene Gebot* ['The Unwritten Commandment'], acrylic on paper and wood, diameter 90 cm, 1996.

Jan Peter Tripp, *Endspiel* ['Endgame'], acrylic on canvas and wood, 50 × 50 cm, 1999.